MW01286542

REVELATION

10WeekBooks.com

REVELATION: A 10 WEEK BIBLE STUDY
3rd Edition

Copyright © 2013 Darren Hibbs
Published by 10 Week Books

Unless otherwise indicated, all Scripture taken from the New King James Version®. Copyright © 1982 by Thomas Nelson, Inc. Used by permission.

Scriptures taken from the Holy Bible, New International Version®, NIV®. Copyright © 1973, 1978, 1984, 2011 by Biblica, Inc.™ Used by permission of Zondervan. All rights reserved worldwide. www.zondervan.com The "NIV" and "New International Version" are trademarks registered in the United States Patent and Trademark Office by Biblica, Inc.™

ISBN: 0988919508
ISBN-13: 978-0-9889195-0-1

Cover: "Four Horsemen of the Apocalypse" by Victor Vasnetsov–Public Domain

10 Week Books
10WeekBooks.com

I dedicate this book to my beautiful wife, Sarah. Your patient endurance, loving acceptance and helping hand make me a better man. You're smart, fun and I've cherished our years together. You are the part of the equation that makes us greater than the sum of our parts.

CONTENTS

ABOUT THE 10 WEEK BIBLE STUDY

My heart is to see people fall in love with God through growing in His Word. The 10 Week Bible Study helps people do that through repetition, helpful commentary and engaging questions. Most of all, this study helps people stay engaged by encouraging them to keep going when they get off track, get confused or get lost.

David, in Psalm 1, told us that if we meditated on God's Word day and night, we would be like a tree planted by rivers of living water. I don't know about you, but I find it hard to remember to meditate at all hours of the day. The 10 Week Bible Study makes that easy by encouraging people to read the book of the Bible being studied 10 times in 10 weeks (hence the name).

When you start reading God's Word like that, you'll find that you accidentally meditate on His Word. In those moments when your mind is at rest and blank, it always snaps to something you've been thinking about. When you pull up to the stoplight, maybe your mind goes to work, chores or that show you've been binging on Netflix lately. With the 10 Week Bible Study, you'll find yourself thinking about God's Word in those moments. You may just catch yourself asking God questions about what you've been reading without even thinking about it.

That is what David meant by meditating on God's Word day and night, that your heart and mind are so full of His Word that you can't help but think about it in those quiet times.

ADDITIONAL RESOURCES

Join the growing community of people who listen, watch and discuss the 10 Week Bible Study online. With millions of downloads and thousands of free resources to choose from, the 10 Week Bible Study produces daily podcasts, videos and other downloadable content to help you grow in your walk with God.

For more information and to join our email list to get regular encouragement in God's Word, visit 10Week-Bible.com today.

OUTLINE OF REVELATION

REVELATION IN 10 WEEKS

REVELATION 1

STUDY QUESTIONS

1. We see right away that the "Revelation" in the book of Revelation is Jesus'. Why is this book Jesus' Revelation?

2. Where was this written from? Why? (see the commentary notes)

3. Revelation was specifically written to the "7 churches of Asia." Who were they? Why was it written to them?

4. Is Revelation still meaningful for us today? If yes, why?

5. What is the meaning of:
    The 7 stars?

    The 7 golden lampstands?

6. Look at the clothing of the man in vs 13-16. Why is He dressed like this?

7. This is Jesus John is describing. How can we be sure this is Jesus?

COMMENTARY NOTES

AUTHOR: JOHN THE APOSTLE

There has been debate about whether or not John, the author of the book of John, wrote Revelation. Even early church historians debated if it was truly John who penned Jesus' Revelation, but the overwhelming majority of historical and modern scholars hold that he did indeed. It's always okay to look at history and tradition with a critical eye, but we must be careful not to overturn them without a preponderance of evidence. In this case, the most likely candidate has and always will be John, the Apostle of the Lamb.

TIME OF WRITING

Most scholars who believe the Bible is God's Word (there are plenty of "scholars" who don't) place the writing around 90 AD, give or take a few years. At this point John is a very old man and is likely the only remaining Apostle of the Lamb alive. He had previously been the bishop (pastor) of a large number of churches centered around the seven churches this letter goes out to.

PURPOSE

The book starts with its purpose--to give us the Revelation of Jesus Christ. It is the revelation that God gave to Jesus about the events of the end time. John spends most of his time with an angelic guide, as we are told in verse 1, but the information of the book is from Jesus, sometimes coming directly from Him. Some have erred by saying this is John's revelation. It isn't. If we are to believe God's Word, then we must understand that the events in Revelation are Jesus' words and not John's commentary on current or future events.

This brings us to an important foundational understanding of Revelation. The revelations belong to Jesus, but the transcription belongs to John. That means it was up to John to write down what he heard and saw. Even though the Holy Spirit directed and guided John's penmanship, we are at a loss to completely understand in human terms a revelation of heavenly origin. That means that some of John's descriptions throughout the book may be vague recollections of something neither he nor anyone he knew had ever seen before. We must be careful not to jump to conclusions as to the surety of our interpretation. Many of the things in this book were most certainly difficult for John to relate to us in the world of finite human understanding.

Verse 3 gives us possibly the most important charge of the book. Read it, listen to it and keep the words written in the book. This is the only such charge given so straight forwardly over any book of the Bible. We are told we are blessed for reading it, for hearing it and especially for keeping it. It is of utmost importance, then, to understand what "keeping" the words of this book means.

Keeping the words of the book certainly involve being well-versed in them--that is having read them over and over and being familiar with what the book actually says versus what common teaching says the book says. We must read, hear and understand this book for ourselves--we can't be satisfied by just believing what another teacher may tell us it says or means.

I personally think that this command to hear also means that we are compelled to actually read the book aloud for those who are illiterate. Illiterate people will be blessed, according to this verse, simply by hearing the words of the book. This means actually reading the text, not basing sermons off the book or passages, but reading the actual words. We see this happening when Ezra read aloud the law to those returning from exile in Babylon (Nehemiah 8). I think this verse gives those of us who are literate the same charge to let people hear the words themselves, not only our interpretation of them.

GREETING

The book is written to the churches of seven of the cities of first century Asia Minor, what is now modern-day western Turkey. There were more churches in Asia at the time, so we must understand that these churches had divine significance to be called out. We also must pause to take into consideration that the book was not only written to those churches, but also to us, now in the 21st century, in America. This may be an easy fact to overlook since we are so accustomed to this practice, but if the book were only written to those churches then they would have no meaning for us today.

While John wrote the letter to these seven churches we will see that the true audience is whoever finds themselves in the events that the book unfolds. It was a common practice of the time to write a letter to a specific audience with full intention of it becoming a "circular" letter, one that was intended to be passed around and read. Revelation is no different. Whereas the specified intended audience were only the churches of seven cities, we can understand that it is to the body of Christ throughout history as a whole, as every other epistle of the New Testament was.

Christ is going to come with the clouds. Everyone on earth will see him, and everyone left on the earth will mourn when they see Him. This is no small clue about this event to come and the New Testament speaks of it many times. Mark 13:26, 1 Thessalonians 4:16-18, 1 Corinthians 15:51-54, & 2 Thessalonians 1:5-7 all reference this even. Daniel also mentions this event in Daniel 7:13-14. This event is what is referenced throughout the Bible as the Great Day of the Lord; or in other places, the Great and Terrible Day of the Lord. We also call this event the Rapture. We'll look in detail later in the book at the concept of the Rapture, but for now know that it is a well-established and very biblical concept.

BEGINNING OF THE VISION

The Island of Patmos is to the west of the coast of modern-day Turkey, which at the time was a predominately Greek-cultured Roman province. (see map on page 3) Tradition tells us that John was the last of the Lamb's apostles alive because all the rest had been martyred. Tradition also tells us that John was also subjected to "attempted" martyrdom, only to miraculously survive. We are told that John was thrown into a vat of boiling oil and survived without any burns or damage to his body. When the officials decided they couldn't kill Jesus' faithful witness, to shut him up they exiled him to Patmos. This claim is hard to verify, but John himself seems to allude to it in the ending of his epistle in John 21:23.

John encounters Jesus while "in the spirit." While this term is vague, we have some hints at what it means through other passages in the Bible. Peter is caught in a trance in Acts 10:10 where he encounters the Lord.

Paul is caught up to the third heaven (God's throne room) in 2 Corinthians 12:1-6 (it is commonly held that Paul is here describing himself). Paul reiterates that he didn't know whether the experience was in the body or out of the body. It must have been such a strange encounter Paul didn't know how to fully explain it. I think what John describes as "being in the spirit" is probably akin to this.

John is commanded to write what he's about to see. I'd be curious to know if he was offered a pen and paper from Jesus or his angel guide or if he was encouraged to hurry and get one while they waited for him. If he wrote with heavenly instruments, what did they look like?

John sees Jesus amongst seven lampstands. The descriptions of Jesus that John gives us are important in the following two chapters as Jesus reveals himself to John here in some of the ways he wants to reveal himself to the seven churches. Some of the interpretations of these symbols we'll look at in chapters 2-3.

For now, we're told the meaning of the seven golden lampstands and the seven stars. The stars are the angels of the churches and the lampstands represent the churches themselves. Many people are intimidated by symbols in Revelation, but often the angel or Jesus himself very plainly explains what the symbols mean.

A note on the angels of the churches: many people are confused by this and find it hard to interpret. Since the meaning of the word angel here is "messenger," many people have interpreted this to mean the pastor of the church.

Whereas this may seem plausible because of other similar references throughout scripture, the intention of this word is exactly how it is translated; "angel." This means that each church has a "guardian" angel, if you will. From books like Daniel, we find that there is a spiritual world that directly correlates to this physical world. Angels and demons are often assigned to geographic locations and have varying levels of authority. Here we are speaking of the seven angels with authority over the seven churches listed in chapters 2-3.

Don't forget to read Revelation this week!
Visit 10WeekBible.com for more resources including daily podcasts, videos and more.

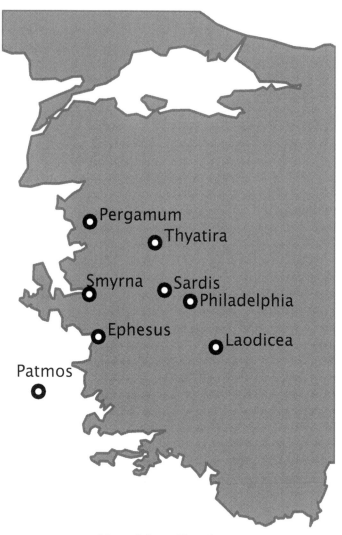

Map of the 7 Churches

REVELATION 2-3

STUDY QUESTIONS

1. How does Jesus introduce Himself to each of the seven churches? Make a summarized list here:

2. What are the promises to the seven churches? Make a list here:

3. Which of the promises are the most meaningful to you? Why?

4. Which church can you see yourself personally in the most? Which can you see your church in?

5. What is the solution to your personal struggles? Your church's?

Which churches received the following

Only Praise	Only Rebuke	Some of Both

COMMENTARY NOTES

The 7 churches of Revelation are one of the most mysteri-ous and challenging parts of the book. There is much con-fusion over the messages, their relevance for inclusion in the book and how they may apply today. There are a lot of cultural implications the message to each church contains that require some careful inspection. The following notes should answer some cursory questions you may have.

Although it may not be immediately apparent, after read-ing through chapters 2-3 many times you will begin to see the patterns and intentions behind the inclusion of these important messages and how they play into the larger nar-rative of Revelation. There is specific information from each church that we need as we interpret the rest of the book; especially the promises Jesus makes to each church.

The messages are definitely just as applicable today as they were to the original recipients. Once we have a small amount of background knowledge we can easily assimilate the concepts herein into our lives.

EPHESUS

Ephesus was an ancient Greco-Roman city on the western Mediterranean shore of modern-day Turkey, then called Asia (Minor). It was home to many different religious sys-tems including Roman deities and the "imperial cult." Its most principal temple was that of the goddess Artemis, as we see in Acts 19:35. Paul spent a great deal of time here evangelizing the entire region around Ephesus. It is be-lieved this is the city that the apostle John lived in with Mary the mother of Jesus until he was exiled.

Ephesus is greeted by Jesus as the one who holds the seven stars and walks among the seven gold lampstands. Remember that from the end of the first chapter the seven stars stand for the seven angels of these churches and that the lampstands represent the churches themselves. Jesus is telling the Ephesians that He is the preeminent authority over the angels and he is walking amongst the churches. He has authority and He is near to us.

Jesus praises the Ephesians for their hard work, enduring hardships patiently and for uncovering false apostles. Then Jesus turns to call Ephesus to repent for becoming wrapped up in their works while forgetting their first love, Him. Possibly one of the most chilling rebukes, Jesus tells the Ephesians that if they don't repent, He will take away their lampstand.

This rebuke probably involves Jesus sending earthly judgment to break up the church so that its members are scattered and there is no more Ephesian church. That may sound like something God would never do to His own church, but He is not intimidated by the idea of his name being slandered at the expense of our hearts growing warm again. Jesus clearly tells the Ephesians here that He would rather have them fully in love with Him than have them exist as a church body that has grown cold. Jesus is willing to disband a church Himself to preserve the hearts of those in attendance.

We know historically that the Ephesians must have taken this warning to heart; because they didn't cease to exist any time shortly after this letter reached them. But the implication is really to us now. As church congregations, we must strive to maintain our love for Jesus or else He will come in and disband our church in one way or another. Think about how many churches you personally know that have "gone under" for one reason or another. Most of the time it is because of finances or the overt sin of a pastor or senior staff. Sometimes churches die off as their population ages and no new evangelism takes place. We normally see that event as something bad, when in fact Jesus is having mercy on those people by scattering them to preserve their hearts to endure until the end.

As for the Nicolaitans, there is no concrete knowledge of who they were or exactly what they taught. The Greek word literally means "destroyer of men." From context later in this chapter we see that it seems they might have taught that lascivious living was acceptable, but that's not certain. Whoever they were, Jesus commends them for standing up against their heresies.

Jesus ends His message to the Ephesians by telling them if they overcome, He will let them eat from the tree of life in the New Jerusalem. We know this is also a promise for us, since the right to eat of that tree is a right granted to every saint as we learn later in this book. The invitation of "who-ever has an ear, let him hear," clues us in that the promises and rebukes were not just to the Ephesians, but also to every believer throughout history.

SMYRNA

Smyrna is a short distance north of Ephesus and was an equally prosperous city of the ancient world. The modern city of Izmir, one of Turkey's largest cities, now encircles the ancient city. Given the context of John's message to the Smyrnians, they obviously faced financial hardships be-cause of their faith in Jesus. How those hardships were caused we don't know, but they definitely suffered.

Smyrna and Philadelphia are the two churches that Jesus has nothing but praise for. Smyrna, however, does receive prophetic insight that they will suffer further for the gospel. Jesus assures them that if they stay faithful even through a short season of persecution, He will give them the crown of life.

Jesus greets Smyrna as the beginning and end and the one who died and rose again. His greeting to them was of comfort, that He has been around before this and He'll be around after this. He also is the one who died, so Jesus is fully aware of their situation and persecution, but He is the one who rose again giving Smyrna, and us, the hope to persevere through persecution.

The Smyrnians may have been poor monetarily, but Jesus bequeaths to them great heavenly wealth for their acts of devotion. There is no better exchange rate than what Jesus offers to those of us who trade earthly wealth in favor of heavenly riches.

The Synagogue of Satan is a curious term. Many have taken this through history to justify horrible things against Jews, but Jesus did not intend it this way. What exactly He meant is not perfectly clear, but it is not an indictment against all Jews. He is most likely speaking of the Jewish leaders of Synagogues who routinely persecuted Christians at this point. We see in Acts that Paul regularly squared off against evil Synagogue leaders who used all manner of lies and manipulation to throw he and others in jail.

Jesus promises them the crown of life if they are faithful unto death. All believers will certainly receive a crown of life, but this may be a special eternal reward for those who overcome in the face of intense persecution. Jesus then offers salvation from the second death to those who overcome; this offering is to everyone who reads this passage, since every saint will be spared the second death, i.e., the lake of fire.

PERGAMUM

Pergamum is the northern-most city of the seven and was a principal city of pagan worship. There were two main centers of worship in Pergamum, other than the imperial cult; the worship of Asclepius and the altar of Zeus. These two centers of worship are worthy of our time to understand since they both still exist today in some form or fashion.

First, the altar of Zeus still exists today in Germany. Every brick of this ancient temple's facade was removed and rebuilt in Berlin. The museum also houses the Ishtar gate of ancient Babylon. Whereas the altar of Zeus wasn't one of the ancient wonders of the world like Ephesus' temple to Artemis, it was a certainly a spiritual stronghold for the area.

Second was the worship of Asclepius. We are told that thousands would come to Pergamum to worship here for its healing powers. Asclepius was the god of snakes and healing. Its symbol is now used by a majority of modern medical professional organizations such as the American Medical Association and the World Health Organization. It is a staff with a single snake wrapped around it. While some people think this is the staff of Moses, it is a reference to the healing power attributed to Asclepius. Some scholars think that Asclepius may have been derived from Moses' staff, since Asclepius was an Egyptian god imported to Greek culture. At Asclepius' temple there were often snakes and drinks of various cures in a very lascivious environment.

On top of these two centers of worship, the imperial cult had a significant foothold, which may give some context to Jesus' message to the church here.

Jesus greets them as himself with the sharp, double-edged sword. This is the same image that we see when Jesus returns at his second coming to kill the wicked assembled against Jerusalem. It is also the symbol of Jesus, the Word of God. He wants those in Pergamum to know He is the one who judges by the Word of God.

Satan's throne may be an implication of one or all of the three various forms of idol worship going on in Pergamum, or it may be a direct inference to where Satan had his earthly throne at the time. We understand that at this point Satan still had access to the heavenly realms, so he was not confined to earth, but Jesus says this twice, so we have no reason to believe that Satan was not himself somehow enthroned here in Pergamum at this time. Even if this weren't the case, anytime Jesus says something twice we should always pay close attention.

Antipas was Jesus' faithful martyr before this satanic stronghold and Jesus calls everyone in Pergamum to stand like Antipas.

Jesus' words of rebuke take us back to the story of Balaam. Many know of the story of his donkey talking (Numbers 22-24), but few know the story of Balaam's sin. After Balaam three times blessed the Israelites instead of cursing them in Numbers 23-24, he is said to have ridden back to his country (presumably on the same donkey that spoke to him). He was stopped along the way by the king's emissaries and brought back with the promise of great wealth to one more time curse Israel.

He finally succumbed to this attempt and told king Balak that if he would send the more beautiful Moabite women to seduce the Israelite chief men into sexual immorality, then they would be persuaded to serve the Moabite gods and in doing so, enrage their own God. In this way, the Moabites would subdue the Israelite army. Balak put this into practice and the Israelites did give into their seductresses and thousands died as a result of God's judgment against them for it.

So, what this means is that there were some in Pergamum saying it was okay to be not only sexually laxed, but encouraging participating in the "sexual revolution" that Pergamum embodied. And again, this is likened to the Nicolaitans, who we perceive taught a similar tolerance of immorality.

Jesus tells those here to repent of their sins or He will come and fight them with the sword in His mouth. He says He will fight them, so it will not be a tender turning to the Lord if they don't repent, but Jesus would judge them harshly with the Word of God.

The church of Pergamum is an especially good example for us today in the Western church. We permit sexual laxity and there are even teachers today who believe it is good. We must today take this to heed and fight against the moral perversion before Jesus comes himself to fight us with the sword of His mouth.

Jesus concludes this with the offering of "hidden manna" and a "white stone" to those who overcome. The hidden manna may be a reference to the great feast of God at the end of the age. "Hidden manna" is curious language, so Jesus may mean something else by this, but we can certainly assume it is good in the same way manna was the gracious provision by God for the children of Israel; provision they didn't have to work for but received each day. In ancient times, white stones were used as tickets into events or as a vote of innocent from a jury (a black stone being cast for guilty), their version of a secret ballot.

THYATIRA

Thyatira had less in the way of pagan worship or persecution from Jewish leaders and was a lesser city of Asia Minor in this day. So the inclusion here may have less to do with a synchronistic culture as outright sinful tolerance. There was a very sexually open lifestyle exhibited in the temples in and around Thyatira, including temple prostitutes.

Jesus introduces himself here as having eyes like fire and bronze feet as we saw in chapter one. He praises them for their works and perseverance, but quickly moves to a lengthy rebuke. They have tolerated Jezebel who called herself a prophetess. She is more than likely not an allusion to Ahab's wife Jezebel, as some have claimed, but an actual woman in Thyatira by this name. She taught people in town that sexual laxity was okay and even encouraged it. Whereas eating food sacrificed to idols wasn't a sin (1 Corinthians 8), she obviously encouraged it in a way that allowed for veneration of the gods it was sacrificed to.

As judgment, God would throw her on a sickbed and kill her children with disease. Since God never judges children for the sin of their fathers this must mean that her literal children were following in her footsteps as teachers or this is a reference to her disciples who followed; not necessarily those just deceived by her teaching. Those who were deceived by her teaching would suffer intensely, but still had time to repent. She and her followers had gone beyond Jesus' patience for their sin. In this way, everyone would see and know that it was God who judged them.

The reference to "Satan's so-called deep secrets" is more than likely a facetious statement. More than likely what Jezebel taught were the "deep secrets" of God that Jesus rightly calls Satan's. Many once-godly teachers have fallen into the same temptation by wanting to teach people the deep things of God only to leave behind the simple teaching of the gospel and holiness. Any time a teacher teaches like this without simple faith and holiness, the enemy is always lurking nearby. Paul warns us to look at our teachers and consider "the outcome of their way of life." (Hebrews 13:7) We must always be discerning.

The pressure to give into this sexual cult must have been so intense in Thyatira that Jesus tells those who have remained pure that they must only hold on to what they have to overcome. He put no other burden of repentance on them; only to stay free of Jezebel's deception.

The overcomers are granted authority over the nations and the morning star. The passage here is a quote here from Psalm 2 about Jesus, but He in turn uses it to give to the saints. Jesus is also called the morning star, but he again offers it to us. Both promises to Thyatira are an offer to rule with Jesus; that we would inherit Him and His reign for eternity.

That is a lofty promise: that the perfect and infinite God would offer to us, His sinful wayward creation, to rule with Him for eternity. This promise alone should stir our emotions with exhilaration. This is where we can understand that we were not only saved *from* hell and punishment, but *to* authority and reigning with Jesus for all eternity. What a wonderful, gracious God we serve!

(I will say of Jezebel, this name is certainly no coincidence, for there are no coincidences with God. Other commenters' references to Ahab's wife could still be valid observations as we can learn from Jezebel's evil as we peer into the world of Revelation. All I am saying is that the name Jezebel is probably referring to an actual woman by that name, not simply an allusion to Old Testament Jezebel)

SARDIS

Jesus introduces Himself here as the one who holds the seven spirits of God and the seven stars. This is a reference to the seven angels of the churches and many believe the Holy Spirit. Sardis was a somewhat decadent city and Jesus has no word of praise for them. Sardis and Laodicea stand alone in stern rebuke.

Jesus says that Sardis is actually dead in the spirit and He calls them to wake up and strengthen what is dying. The chilling thing here is that Sardis had a reputation for being alive. This should give us pause for reflection. Just because men say we are thriving and alive doesn't mean God is of the same opinion. We should always strive to live and view ourselves in whatever manner God would judge us by, not by the praise or rebuke of man.

"Perfect" is an interesting word here Jesus uses to describe the works of those in Sardis. We should think about this term in context to God's thoughts on perfection. If we understand that we have no fleshly path to perfection we conclude that our only method of perfection is through Jesus' redemption. So what it seems like Jesus is saying is that Sardis (and all of us) must throw ourselves into the salvation and grace of Jesus to obtain a perfect work. Good deeds and works outside of this will always fail God's test of perfection.

To those who haven't soiled their robes in the spiritual complacency of Sardis, Jesus promises that they would be clothed in white. Again, this is a promise to all saints as we see later in Revelation. Jesus will acknowledge these over-comers before the Father and His angels and leave their names in the book of life; again, a promise to all believers.

PHILADELPHIA

Jesus gives only praise to Philadelphia, and lots of it. He introduces himself here as holy and true and holding David's key. This is a messianic prophecy from Isaiah 22:22.

The back-story here is when the king of Assyria camped outside Jerusalem, king Hezekiah sent his palace servants Shebna and Eliakim to Isaiah to find out if they would be destroyed by Assyria (2 Kings 19). Isaiah prophesied that they would not even have to fight them, but the Lord used the opportunity before these two men to point out that Shebna would be disgraced and die in a foreign land while Eliakim would be granted the high place in his master Hezekiah's house and the key of David.

This key sounds a lot like the promise Jesus gives in Matthew 18:18 speaking of all believers' authority in com-munal prayer. Whatever we bind on earth will be bound in heaven and vice-versa. Wherever we join two or more in prayer God will hear and act as if we carried the authority of heaven. This is truly a powerful promise.

Jesus again brings up this Synagogue of Satan, but this time He tells the Philadelphians that they will be vindicated be-fore them. Jesus also promises them safety and security from the hour of trial that is coming. This is a reference to the great tribulation. There is protection from the great tribulation for some saints as we will find later in this book, but here Jesus specifically tells the ones who have faithfully endured that they will be protected. This would seem to be a challenge to the idea that the saints will all be raptured before the start of the great tribulation. We will deal with this more in depth later in the book.

The promise to Philadelphia overcomers is to be made a pillar in the temple of God. They will also have God's name written on them, as contrasted to the name of the antichrist as we will see later, and the name of the New Jerusalem, as contrasted with the name of the city of Babylon, and they will receive Jesus' new name.

These are interesting promises since John tells us that in the eternal city of Jerusalem there is no physical temple. Revelation 21:22 tells us that God Himself is the temple. Several times in Revelation we are faced with this paradoxical challenge: we will be servants and pillars in God's temple, but only God Himself will be the temple for eternity. Forever there will be no formal rituals or rites to come before the presence of the Almighty; we will see Him face-to-face for eternity and live in His tangible presence.

LAODICEA

There is nothing but rebuke for this cold, stale church. Jesus proclaims He is the faithful and true witness, the ruler of creation. We understand through Laodicea's rebuke that the church thought of herself as rich, but was just the opposite before Jesus. As with Sardis, it is God's opinion we should care about, not man's. We can learn a lot from this rebuke as it closely mirrors the state of the Western church today. Not cold, not hot, but lukewarm. Wealth and contentment clouded the vision of this church, and so it does our church today, of our true nakedness.

Jesus addresses Laodicea as the Faithful and True witness and the Beginning of the creation of God. He is laying out clearly His authority to instruct and correct Laodicea. It's as if Jesus is making His case why His opinion matters more than the voices Laodicea has been listening to instead.

The comfort to Laodicea is that God is rebuking them because He loves them. Jesus does not rebuke those outside the fold of salvation the same as He does those that are His. Like a father disciplining his child, God moves us to repentance. Even though Laodicea receives one of the strongest rebukes directly from God in scripture there is still room to repent and be made right before a loving and gracious God. We serve that same God today.

If the Laodiceans overcome, they are promised the right to sit with Jesus on his throne. This is similar to what saints are offered in the millennial kingdom, to rule with Jesus on the earth. Like the promise to Thyatira this one should stir our hearts to be undone by the great grace and faithfulness of God. Our sins rightly deserve eternal separation and punishment but instead God gives the right to sit and judge to the redeemed. We must carefully consider what the writer of Hebrews called "so great a salvation." (Hebrews 2:3)

Don't forget to read Revelation this week!
Visit 10WeekBible.com for more resources including daily podcasts, videos and more.

REVELATION 4-5

STUDY QUESTIONS

1. In chapter 4, who is dressed in white with crowns on their heads?

2. Who else has described the four living creatures? What was different about his description?

3. Why is God worthy? Why is it important for us to realize God is worthy for the same reasons? How can we live our lives with this reality in mind?

4. What is the scroll? Why is Jesus the only one who can take the scroll?

5. Why is Jesus described as a Lion and a Lamb in the same passage?

6. Why do the creatures and the elders have harps and bowls? What do the bowls represent?

7. What does it mean that the Lamb has seven horns and seven eyes? Why would it be important for us to know things that aren't clearly explained?

COMMENTARY NOTES

THRONE ROOM

As in Isaiah 6, Ezekiel 3 and 2 Corinthians 12, John has been taken to the Lord's throne room. John gives us the most detailed description of this place throughout Revelation than any other scripture writer. John was commanded at the beginning of Revelation to write what he sees and hears, something very different than any other Biblical writer. Others who had been taken to the throne room or shown future events were only given smaller and dimmer pieces of the puzzle, but John appears to be seeing things very clearly. Instead of being given the vision for some specific purpose, God seems to be pulling back the veil for all to see what heaven currently looks like and what eternity will be through John's writing.

To be certain, John is only writing the main points of his encounter. I'm sure if he were to have written in detail everything he saw, Revelation alone would double the length of the Bible. John has only written down what was important to God to be conveyed to us, which means we should definitely take seriously everything written in the book.

John describes the living creatures having six wings, just like Ezekiel (Ezekiel 1), but he says they have eyes everywhere. John also leaves out "Ezekiel's wheel" they seem to ride around on. Both speak of them crying "Holy" about the Lord. The twenty-four thrones of the elders beg some questions, though. Who were they? Are they angels, or humans? This question is never answered. Some say it is the twelve patriarchs of Israel and the twelve apostles. If this isn't John the beloved (the apostle of the Lamb), then that could be a realistic explanation, but it would seem perplexing for John the Revelator to be one of the twenty-four elders. Either way, we are not given their identity; only that they exist.

The elders are clothed in white and wear crowns, which suggests that they are humans, since no other reference to crowns is given except to those who have earned them from earthly deeds. That is not to say, though, that the Lord couldn't have given them to angels, etc. So in the end we are still left with possibly more questions than we have answers for. What we do know for sure about the four living creatures and the 24 elders is that we are introduced to them here because they will all have significant authority over the events that will transpire throughout the rest of the book.

The description of the throne room conjures up images of the tabernacle of Moses and Solomon's temple. Things like the altar and the sea of glass are directly represented in these two ancient representations of God's realm. David even told us that He saw this place, as God gave him the designs for Solomon's temple in 1 Chronicles 28:19.

The Father is enthroned in a room described by John with colors of gems; red, crystal and surrounded by a rainbow with a green-tint. John's description should be seen as the best he could describe with the words he had. To describe God's throne as resembling an earthly gem is probably less than realistic. If we had been there, we probably all would have struggled just as much with how to describe how it looked.

JESUS TAKES THE SCROLL

The scroll that the Father has in His right hand is the plan for the end of this age. This is the Revelation of Jesus Christ that God gave Him that John spoke of in chapter 1. It is interesting that Jesus is described as the Lion and the Lamb in the same moment when it comes time for Him to take the scroll. He is worthy because He overcame and will rule and because He was slain for our sins. We are told explicitly that the seven horns and eyes on the lamb are the seven spirits (or Holy Spirit) of God.

These seven horns, eyes and spirits of God are something that is a complete mystery to most commentators. We don't find anything like this anywhere else in scripture. We can make conjecture from other places in scripture, but nothing is certain. We must understand that God had purpose for us to know this information without fully understanding it now.

This is an important reality for us to grasp about Revelation: God has not made all the things in the book immediately understandable. Some things will only be revealed in time. Whereas we truly can understand much of what's in the book, there are a few things that conjecture and speculation will not give us: we need direct revelation from God. We'll see later in Revelation where God specifically withholds interpretation but gives us a sneak peak into something going on (Revelation 10:4). In time, God will reveal these things even if only as they happen.

The takeaway is that Jesus is worthy to take the scroll because He created all things and then was slain for us (Lion and Lamb) and He is part of the trinity of the all-seeing and all-knowing God.

Jesus taking the scroll is a very big deal, as all heaven erupts in the greatest worship song in history. Even the earth joins in the song.

Song to Jesus & Prayers of the Saints

5:8 is a verse that harkens back to the "tabernacle (tent) of David." (Amos 9:11) David's fallen tent in Amos referenced not only the nation of Israel but also specifically "Davidic worship." This was a model of 24/7 worship and prayer outlined in 1 Chronicles 25 and clearly mimicking the worship going on in heaven from the creatures and elders. This around the clock worship went on for decades or possibly centuries before it stopped. It has been reinstituted throughout Christian history and is now a growing movement as seen in places like South Korea, parts of Europe and in America as part of the International House of Prayer movement.

The elders and living creatures are holding harps and bowls that symbolize the saints' worship (harps) and prayers (bowls filled with incense). The prayers of the saints come up again later in Revelation. In this case, it seems that the saints' prayers are what releases the Seal judgments. In Chapter 8, it is clear that the prayers of the saints release judgment, so it's an interesting thing to think that the saints will be the people who release the seal judgments, fully knowing what they mean and hold in store for them.

As we'll learn later in Revelation, the reason the saints pray for the release of these judgments is the pressure put on them by Babylon and the Harlot's system of religion and her economy. It's not the Antichrist who first persecutes Christians, but Babylon and the Harlot. As we'll see later in the book, the Harlot can primarily be understood as a system of religion and economy, while it seems Babylon is a real city, most probably a rebuilt city on or near the site of ancient Babylon.

The Harlot system and Babylon will so persecute Christians and the world will have turned so far into wickedness that the saints on earth will in unison cry out for Jesus to take the scroll and release its seals. The saints will be praying for justice on the earth and Jesus will be the only one left to turn to for it.

The elders and creatures again cry out in song, this time joined by innumerable angels. This song eclipses the worship song sung in the previous chapter. All heaven and earth are now ready for Jesus to return and take His rightful place as ruler of heaven AND earth. The sequence of events in chapter 5 set in motion Jesus' return to rule for 1,000 years. The following three series of judgments will purify the earth from all the wickedness in it. Everyone allied with Babylon and the Antichrist will die in the coming years as Jesus returns.

Don't forget to read Revelation this week!
Visit 10WeekBible.com for more resources including daily podcasts, videos and more.

REVELATION 6-7

STUDY QUESTIONS

1. Why do you think the four living creatures are speaking the words to release the first four judgments? What does this say about God's sharing of authority in heaven?

2. What is the rider in Seal one holding? What is he not holding? Why might this be important?

3. What other passage of scripture sounds like Seal two (refer to commentary)? What must change (be taken out of the way) before Seal 2 can happen?

4. How many calories a day do you eat? If you have a family, how many calories a day do you eat as a whole? List a daily meal plan for you or your family that would equal 2,600 calories:

5. How many people live in your town? What would ¼ of the population dying in a nine-month period do to its infrastructure/economy/psyche?

6. How is Seal 5 a judgment? Why do the people acknowledge God in seal 6?

7. Who are the 144,000 in Revelation 7? Why is this list interesting?

8. What is our promise in Revelation 7 to those who overcome this terrible time?

COMMENTARY NOTES

The prelude to the seals opens with God the Father, sitting on His throne, holding a scroll in His right hand. The scroll is written on both sides, sealed with seven seals. This is much like the scroll Ezekiel is told to eat in Ezekiel 2:8-10.

Bound books didn't come about until a century or so after John died. Whereas it is not impossible for this to be what he observed, the connotation seems to suggest it was indeed a scroll, something John was used to seeing. The scroll was rolled up with seven wax seals, which Jesus pulls off one by one.

Seals 1-4 are packaged together in an interesting format. They are a common series, just as the first four trumpet judgments and bowl judgments are different from the last three of each series. The first four seal judgments should be understood as the rise of the Antichrist's government. That may seem to go against God's nature to be the one who releases the Antichrist, but what is actually happening is God is granting him authority. We find out later that it is actually God who has given him this direct authority (Revelation 13:7)

FIRST SEAL

Given the language John uses consistently throughout the book, we understand that Jesus (the lamb) is the one opening the seals. Jesus is opening the seals, but the living creatures are the ones giving direction to what John is seeing. It's as if each of the four living creatures are assigned to administer one of the first four seals. Each of the first four seals is ramping up to the fourth which concludes with ¼ of the population of the earth dying within a very short period of time.

To view Jesus as the rider of the first horse of the seal judgments would require adjusting the interpretation of many other facets of Revelation, which makes it unlikely for this passage to be speaking of Jesus. The 21 judgments happen in order, and Jesus' return does not come until the end of the 21st judgment, the last bowl. To place Jesus into the context of the rider of the white horse would not make sense here, so it must be someone else.

Taking the clues we're given from other passages of scripture (Daniel 9:27, Zechariah 19) it seems clear that the rider of the horse is the Antichrist (or something symbolizing his new government). He will ride in on a white horse like a savior with a bow. The bow speaks of no arrows, making one think that there will be little or no bloodshed in his rise to power. Daniel seems to allude to this as well in that the Antichrist will confirm a covenant at the beginning of the last 7 years. Later in Revelation we'll see that ten nations willingly give him their authority, so no war may be needed for the Antichrist to rise to power.

It may seem against God's nature for Him to be the one to release the Antichrist, but it is in fact one of the most important aspects of Revelation for us to properly understand. We will deal with Babylon later in the book, but the Antichrist's role is to usurp and bring complete judgment upon the wicked Harlot Babylon. God wants us to understand from Revelation that this evil that's brewing will be the worst thing in history.

Just as God used Babylon to subdue and purify His people once before, He will do it again. And just like Babylon's overnight destruction by Persia, God will raise up a leader who will destroy and judge Babylon again. That leader will be the Antichrist. (Daniel 5, Isaiah 44-49)

SECOND SEAL

Here again, John is told by a second living creature to look at what's happening. We clearly see that since these seals are numbered, they are happening sequentially. Seal two takes place after seal one and before seal three.

It can be understood here that the rider is again the Antichrist (or a symbol of his government). Even if the rider is not the Antichrist, whoever it is is going to cause worldwide unrest. Murder is going to increase here and wars and the tensions of worldwide war will begin to build. The tensions are rising and they'll come to a catastrophic head in the fourth seal.

Paul tells us that God is restraining sin in the world until the time when He will release the Antichrist.

> *6And now you know what is restraining, that he may be revealed in his own time. 7For the mystery of lawlessness is already at work; only He who now restrains will do so until He is taken out of the way. 8And then the lawless one will be revealed, whom the Lord will consume with the breath of His mouth and destroy with the brightness of His coming.*
>
> *2 Thessalonians 2:6-8*

What we see in the second seal sounds a lot like this restraint has been taken away, lending support to the rider in seal one being the Antichrist.

THIRD SEAL

Worldwide famine of this order is quite a frightening event. A denarius is a day's wages for one man. So, what this is saying is that one full day's work will buy around 2,600 calories of wheat (roughly what is contained in both a quart of wheat and 3 quarts of barley).

That's the daily recommended caloric intake for a grown man for a day. That means that a family of four would have to split that amount of food, every day; which means 650 calories per person per day. Anything less than 1,000 calories a day is not sustainable for very long. Diseases and disorders from malnutrition would begin to set in quickly.

So does this mean that 100% of the earth's population is suffering without food? No. The wealthy and powerful will certainly still have their luxuries, as hinted at by "do not harm the oil and the wine." Those with the power to do so will allow others to die from hunger so they can continue living lavishly. History has shown this to be true and it will not change in the third seal.

Some saints and different geographic regions will be spared from this judgment to varying extents, however. There is surely some area of the globe producing food during this period, and just like in Egypt under Joseph there will be supply.

This is a good time to take a step back and think about the plagues of Egypt. The plaques of Revelation are intended to conjure images in our minds of those the Israelites went through before Moses led them to freedom. In Egypt, they increased in intensity until God freed His people under great judgment of the wicked.

So it will be in Revelation: these judgments will increase in intensity until God gives ultimate and eternal freedom to His people from this wicked world. And just as in Egypt, we will also later see that there will be a place (or places) of peace and safety for God's people as there was in Goshen.

As believers, we must keep in mind that these plaques are not intended for us because, *"God did not appoint us to wrath, but to obtain salvation through our Lord Jesus Christ,"* (1 Thessalonians 5:9). God's wrath was not intended for the Israelites in Egypt and neither will His wrath be aimed at us in these terrible times.

FOURTH SEAL

Ezekiel 14:21 is the exact four things listed in the fourth seal. Ezekiel goes on to speak about the sorrow and comfort that will come about after this destruction. Ezekiel alludes to these plagues causing massive death. He says that there will be a remnant. A remnant means that it will seem like everyone is going to die, but that the death will stop.

> *21For thus says the Lord God: "How much more it shall be when I send My four severe judgments on Jerusalem—the sword and famine and wild beasts and pestilence—to cut off man and beast from it? 22Yet behold, there shall be left in it a remnant who will be brought out, both sons and daughters; surely they will come out to you, and you will see their ways and their doings. Then you will be comforted concerning the disaster that I have brought upon Jerusalem, all that I have brought upon it. 23And they will comfort you, when you see their ways and their doings; and you shall know that I have done nothing without cause that I have done in it," says the Lord God.*

Ezekiel 14:21-23

The fourth seal is easily the most catastrophic judgment to hit the earth yet. In a very short period of time, ¼ of the earth will die by unnatural causes. War, famine, disease and wild animals will take the lives of a quarter of the population of the earth "before their time." This won't just be big news, it will be the only news for some time. This will for sure begin to eclipse every Hollywood Apocalyptic movie ever made. But, as we see in Ezekiel, even during the real Apocalypse God will send His mercy on the earth.

Of the four causes of death in this seal, the last is by far the most puzzling. One can easily imagine how war, famine and disease could take billions of lives, but how can wild animals kill a significant part of earth's population? In perspective, if each of these four things kills a ¼ of the ¼ of the population being killed (although it doesn't say that), then the number of people killed by wild animals would be 500 million people (if the world population was 8 billion). It is unthinkable right now how wild animals could kill a half a billion people. Rest assured that something is coming that is going to change the natural order of things and men will no longer be feared by the animal kingdom as is the case today.

In case you missed the math, ¼ of the earth's population (assuming 8 billion people) would be 2 billion. Take a moment to think of what the reality of 2 billion people suddenly dying in their prime would do to planet earth. The time frame of this is probably only a few months up to a year. That kind of rapid death is enough to bring the world to its knees.

FIFTH SEAL

If each of the judgments is increasing in intensity, why does the fifth seal seem to be taking a step backwards? At first glance, this seems to be a pronouncement to the martyred saints that their living counterparts will have it worse for a while. Whereas the first four judgments are fairly easy to analyze on their own, seals five and six need to be read in context of the first four.

The first four seals, trumpet and bowl judgments are similar in their pattern. They quickly lay the foundation for the remaining three judgments in their series to take place, which are markedly different in type, albeit much worse. Even though seal five may not seem much worse, it is by far the harshest of the seal judgments against the wicked of planet earth yet.

General Yamamoto of Japan famously said, "We have now awakened a sleeping giant," in reference to attacking Pearl Harbor in World War II before officially declaring war on America. The Japanese resolve didn't immediately fade, but it quickly became apparent who the losing nation was going to be. The same is true of seal five. The first four judgments were centered around the Antichrist's system judging the earth for the Harlot Babylon's reign of terror on the earth. Now, God is asked to turn His attention to the Antichrist and the proverbial sleeping giant is awakened.

Although Jesus was not sleeping, His actions here say something big. He gives those martyrs of the tribulation white clothes to wear. It seems that every other saint receives these clothes at the resurrection, but to these saints they receive them now and Jesus gives them a promise that their justice is swiftly coming. In Deuteronomy 9:4-6, God very sternly tells the Israelites that He wasn't giving them the land of Canaan because of their own righteousness, but because of the wickedness of its current inhabitants. God told Abram (Abraham) in Genesis 15:16 that the land would be his descendants' after 400 years because the sin of the Amorites wasn't yet complete. In both cases, Genesis AND Revelation, God was unwilling to judge a people because of someone else's righteousness, but only for a people's own wickedness.

Whereas the Israelites were judged unrighteous in Deuteronomy 9, the saints in the fifth seal are judged righteous by their white garments. Both, however, are given the same word from Jesus: wait. One human's righteousness can never be compared to another's; Jesus is the only righteous standard by which mankind can be judged and Jesus is giving men on earth in the fifth seal more time to repent or continue in their sin.

Even though Jesus' word is "wait," the earth will very shortly tremble from the passionate execution of this request of vindication by Jesus, as we'll see in the sixth seal.

SIXTH SEAL

Although the full release of Jesus' judgment against the wicked will not be fully realized until the seventh bowl judgment, the martyred saints in heaven don't have to wait long to see Jesus give a down payment on his promise to vindicate them in the fifth seal.

Interestingly, this seal judgment changes the nature of the judgments away from man-made and man-involved judgments to those created by the natural order: the earth, sky and cosmic disturbances. From here on out, every judgment will no longer involve man's hand to carry out, but things beyond man's control. This is no small detail.

This is also the beginning of the total fulfillment of Joel 2. There's an earthquake, the sun is obscured (more than likely by volcanic debris, etc., but also possibly by an eclipse), the moon goes through a lunar eclipse (blood moon) and meteors/meteorites are falling to the earth (more than just the annual Leonid meteor showers). Mountains and islands are shaken and there are disturbances in the sky.

Whereas we would like to think that we understand the science of the earth and the heavens better than our ancient ancestors, all these events in close proximity to each other will have everyone on the planet scrambling for literal caves because of the perils of these omens of disaster.

They will also correctly understand them as omens from an angry God. It won't change their course, however, as we'll see from here out.

DIVINE PROTECTION

Chapter 7 gives us our first glimpse of some of the people (not all) that the Lord has hand-picked to endure the tribulation with some level of safety. This chapter is divided into two sections; the 144,000 of Israel and the saints from all people groups (ethnos, in Greek).

144,000 SEALED

This number and its meaning is viewed by very few people today as literal because of many misconceptions. For one reason or another, many interpreters' theological prejudices keep them from seeing this as literally 12,000 from each of the tribes of actual Israel like John describes. Many people try to explain this away as "spiritual Israel" as Paul alludes to in Romans, which would be the Gentile church. Others see this as some sort of hidden meaning much deeper than the passage supplies because of the exactness of the numbers totaling 144,000. Cults have been started (Jehovah's Witnesses) based on this passage.

To be sure, the words mean what they say. 144,000 Jews from Israel will be separated and spared the fate of everyone else in the great tribulation. They are not promised that they won't suffer hunger or cold, but that they won't be killed. We don't know what their lives will look like during the tribulation, only that they will survive it.

The list is far too precise not to be taken literally. Instead of resting on the statement in verse 4 that some from every tribe of Israel will be sealed, the angel lists for John the twelve tribes by name.

The tribes listed here should be closely examined. They are different from any other listing in the Bible. The tribes of Dan and Ephraim have been excluded while Joseph has been included even though Manasseh is also.

Every other listing where Levi is included lists only Joseph, and others where Levi is excluded (because they had no physical inheritance in Israel) always list Manasseh and Ephraim instead of Joseph, since Jacob reckoned Joseph's two children as his own when he arrived in Egypt. (Ephraim and Manasseh were often listed as 2 of the twelve tribes in lieu of Joseph being a single tribe. They were often called the "half-tribes")

The reason many have a hard time with this list is because 9 of the tribes of Israel were "lost" when the northern kingdom of Israel was carried away captive by Assyria. Only Judah, Levi and Benjamin survived since they were carried away captive to Babylon and allowed to return.

We can't comprehend how this list could work since Jews don't know their tribal affiliation anymore, but that shouldn't cause us not to believe what the Word says. Many have incorrectly interpreted throughout history that every reference to Israel in Revelation must be figurative of the church because they couldn't conceive of Israel ever being a nation again. 1948 proved them wrong when Israel became a recognized nation. The listing of tribes should be taken literally as Jews who have accepted Jesus as their Messiah and not some symbol of the Gentile church or any other manner of interpretation. It's always better to believe what the Bible says instead of trying to come up with a convenient interpretation to suit our prejudices.

INNUMERABLE SAINTS

This passage is the fulfillment of Jesus' prophecy from Matthew 24:14 that people from "all nations" will hear the gospel of the kingdom. Every people group from the earth is represented in the second half of chapter 7. This is a beautiful passage about the completion of our task to disciple people from every nation and tongue. Jesus promises here that we will complete it and that we will live forever with Him in eternity.

There is a troubling part of this passage that is easy to overlook. Verse 16 tells us that these saints who have died during the great tribulation will have suffered hunger and scorching heat. This sounds a lot like people who have been forced to survive in concentration camps. It seems reasonable, given history, that scores of Jews and sympathetic Gentile Christians will live out many of their last days in concentration camps like those of Nazi Germany. Or worse.

Zechariah 14 alludes to this kind of treatment of Jews in Jerusalem. Gentiles who stand with the Jewish people will certainly meet the same fate as those who did during World War II.

Having a prepared heart will be important for everyone who must endure this time in history. We are clearly promised, however, that we who endure until the end will be forever rewarded with white robes and will rest with Jesus. Our conduct and works while here on this earth really do matter.

No matter what we may suffer for a short period of time it will be worth it for eternity. Revelation is a very scary book for many people because of the terrible judgments, but we must remember that they are not intended for us. This chapter is about God's provision and proclamation of victory over His saints. We are told, however, that we will suffer. In the same way that the Israelites suffered at the hand of Pharaoh (not the judgments), so we are told we will suffer at the hand of the Antichrist.

We may be exiled, forced into concentration camps or executed, but Jesus promises us He will see it all and it's worth it. Revelation is in part God's mercy to us by telling us a painful truth of times to come. It will certainly be the worst time the earth has ever endured, but Christians will not be taken by surprise by it.

Jesus' words in Matthew 24 reiterate this point. We should take comfort that God will see and reward us for all our suffering that we may endure. He is for us and in the end He assures us eternal victory.

> *"See, I have told you beforehand."*
>
> *Matthew 24:25*

Don't forget to read Revelation this week!
Visit 10WeekBible.com for more resources including daily
podcasts, videos and more.

REVELATION 8-9

STUDY QUESTIONS

1. Why would the saint's prayers play an active role in releasing judgment? Why do you think the saints would be asking for God to judge the earth at this point?

2. List some things you think would happen as a result of ⅓ of all the earth's trees and all the grass being burned up.

3. What countries would be most affected by the sea being struck (sea life, shipping, etc.)? How would this affect your day-to-day life if it happened today?

4. How does losing ⅓ of earth's fresh water further complicate things? How would you deal with this?

5. List some things you think would happen if ⅓ of the light of day disappeared. What theory can you come up with as to how this could possibly happen?

6. Who do you think this army of 200 million is? How do you think people would be prohibited from taking their own lives?

7. What would your city look like if now ½ of its population were dead? How would it carry on? Why do you think everyone isn't turning to God?

COMMENTARY NOTES

As the last seal is opened, we see the prayers of the saints play a pivotal role in releasing these next judgments. The cork is off, and now the judgments of God begin to flow out of the bowl of His wrath with increasing intensity, but not completely. We've also transitioned away from any events caused by man to events that are completely outside the realm of human interaction (comets striking earth, etc.).

SEVENTH SEAL

Jesus opens the seventh seal and there is silence in heaven. This is one of the most perplexing things in all Revelation. I'm not sure what silence in heaven will look like for those of us on earth, or how long "half an hour" means--whether literal or figurative. This reminds me of when Solomon dedicated the Temple in 2 Chronicles 7:1-2. God put a stop to everything in the temple, even the things He'd ordained, so that those there would experience a holy moment. This seems a lot like that.

Like the release of the seal judgments, the prayers of the saints again play a role in releasing the trumpet judgments. This time the prayers of the saints are filled into a bowl that is given to an angel who hurls it to earth and causes a great shaking to the atmosphere and the earth itself. Seal judgments 6 and 7 have both included earthquakes.

The most important thing to note about seal 7 is that it releases the trumpet judgments.

FIRST TRUMPET

We now begin the judgment of thirds. In the seal series, ¼ of the earth's population was killed. Now God increases the intensity to affect ⅓ of the remaining population of the earth. A third of all the trees are burned up by hail and fire mixed with blood. What exactly two of these three things really are is debatable, but hail most certainly means hail. What I mean by that is that hail is what is produced by weather patterns of swirling, strong winds with an updraft strong enough to create balls of ice that eventually become too heavy for the wind and fall to earth. John knew what hail was, so the inclusion of that here certainly means literal hail. There's no reason to take this figuratively.

Now, as to what causes this hail is unknown. It could possibly be a storm system or some other system capable of producing hail that we've never seen before. This will certainly be unprecedented because we've never before seen a hail storm that could burn things up, and certainly not to the tune of ⅓ of the earth's trees and all its green grass. How fire and blood are mixed in or even what that looks like is a mystery.

What's not a mystery is that this will have a devastating impact on the people of the earth. Imagine smoke circling the planet from the fires, the devastation of homes, etc. and the amount of increased carbon dioxide in the atmosphere from the smoke and lack of trees to soak up that CO_2 (there you go, Al Gore). Earth itself is beginning to become an unpleasant place to be.

SECOND TRUMPET

This to me sounds like a comet or huge meteorite. It too will have the devastating impact that all the doomsday scientists say it would. The celestial object is thrown into the sea and ⅓ of all sea life dies, and ⅓ of all the ships are destroyed. Where this is going to impact to have this effect is unknown, but the consequences are staggering.

Water being turned to blood like in the days of Egypt sounds hard to take literally, but we just don't know what this will look like. As in the case of a "blood moon" (the ancients' way of describing a lunar eclipse), this may be a figurative description of water turning red and deadly. No matter how it actually happens, the water will kill whatever's in it.

Whereas many people in the United States do not live off the sea as a way of life, many hundreds of millions of people worldwide do. The sea will be turned to blood and everything in it will be completely unusable. Global trade will be dramatically interrupted as ⅓ of the earth's shipping is instantly eliminated.

THIRD TRUMPET

"Star" to the ancients meant any illuminated heavenly body. The word "planet" is from the Greek word meaning "wanderer" because they called them "wandering stars." That is because they move across the field of fixed stars and constellations in the sky. Before telescopes, planets looked no different in the night sky except that some of them are brighter than some stars.

So, with that understanding we know that John is telling us some illuminated body that is observable from earth will strike the land now. That may be a comet or a large meteorite. We don't know, but it will again have devastating effect. Whatever this object is, it somehow does not cause a devastating impact by itself, but it's contents poison the fresh water of earth. Imagine if ⅓ of all the fresh water on the planet was instantly gone. Water is already scarce in densely populated places now so this will make life on earth difficult for its residents. ¼ of the earth gone missing from the seal judgments has already taxed earth's infrastructure; God is increasing the pressure to get men's attention.

FOURTH TRUMPET

However this happens, we're meant to understand that losing a third of our light will literally take place and that its effects will be greater in intensity than the previous three judgments. It's possible that the days and nights will be ⅓ shorter, or that something will obscure the vision from earth into space. Whatever the cause, the imagination wanders to think of what life will look like and how it will change.

How will crops grow with a third less light? Will this increase famine? Places like Seattle that receive rain most of the year cause people to become depressed. After all that's happened, what will this loss of light do to the psyche of earth's inhabitants?

THE THREE WOES

When an angel tells us that things are about to get even worse than what they already have been, it must be serious. Whether this will be an event seen by humans or whether we'll know prophetically that this angel has sounded his warning we can't be sure. We can be sure that the saints still alive on earth will know when this happens.

FIFTH TRUMPET

Again John calls the thing that falls from heaven a star, but this time he associates it with a being. He says that this star was given a key, so this must be symbolic in some way. Perhaps the star falling to earth is real and signals these events, or it could be that the "star" is the Bible's word for an angel as we've seen in chapter 1 and as we'll see again later in the description of Satan and his demons in 12:4.

The locusts' identity is something for the imagination. It's obvious they're bad, and they've been released by a "fallen angel" named "Destroyer" so many interpreters believe they are demonic in some way. Some have said this is John's best description at his time of a helicopter, but these still seem other-worldly even by today's standards. This is definitely a place where I'm sure John was at a loss to accurately describe something he'd never seen before. Just like John's description of the four living creatures, we're offered a literary description of something that can probably only be fully understood through seeing.

Whatever they actually are, we do know several important facts for sure. First, we know that we as the saints will not be harmed by them. Only those without the seal of God will be harmed. Secondly, we know this will last for exactly five months. Third, we know this will be so horrible that everyone affected will want to die, but for some reason won't be able to.

Because of the mystery of the events and the extreme nature of this judgment, it certainly sounds like the worst thing to happen so far. But we're again warned that the following two judgments are by far worse.

SIXTH TRUMPET

Four angels have been bound at the Euphrates River and waiting for this moment their entire existence, so it seems, to release these devastating horsemen. Again, many commentators see these horses and horsemen as demonic while others see this as John's best attempt to describe some modern technological army. Whatever they are, the clues we're given will be important someday. Since seal 6 all the judgments have had an "otherworldly" sense to them, so it may be a good idea not to rush too quickly to understand these horsemen as human.

John must have been taken aback by the sheer number of these creatures. He wouldn't have known it, but at the time of his writing this book there weren't 200 million people on planet earth. At any rate, they kill ⅓ of the remaining population of the earth. That means that by the sixth trumpet, ½ of the earth's population has died prematurely in a very short period of time; 3.5 years or less. (¼ + ⅓ = ½) This is actually what Jesus is speaking of here in Luke:

> *34I tell you, in that night there will be two men in one bed: the one will be taken and the other will be left. 35Two women will be grinding together: the one will be taken and the other left. 36Two men will be in the field: the one will be taken and the other left."*
>
> *37And they answered and said to Him, "Where, Lord?" So He said to them, "Wherever the body is, there the eagles will be gathered together."*

> *Luke 17:34-37*

Many people interpret this as the rapture, but Jesus is clearly talking about dead people, not people who have disappeared. In Luke 17:37 Jesus answers his disciples that the events of the last day will be evident because of the dead bodies that eagles (or vultures in some translations: they are carrion-eating birds) have gathered around. The "one taken and one left" means that ½ of the earth will have died in a very short time period.

We can infer from the way in which the seals and trumpets unfold that the seals occupy more of the last 3-½ years of time than do the trumpets. If we were to guess at that timing, we might say that in a 2 to 3-year span of time the seals unfold and in 9-18 months the trumpets take place. What this means is that now ⅓ of the earth has died even more rapidly than in the seals.

The chapter concludes by saying that after all of the judgments, those bound in sin did not repent of their wickedness. The list of sinful deeds is important to note. Often in the West we equate idol worship to things like television or football, but it is clear here that actual idols will be worshipped again worldwide. There will also be a great increase in murder, witchcraft, sexual immorality and theft, which we have already seen increasing.

Don't forget to read Revelation this week!
Visit 10WeekBible.com for more resources including daily podcasts, videos and more.

REVELATION 10-11

STUDY QUESTIONS

1. Why would God want us to know about these "seven thunders" but keep from us what they said?

2. What is the mystery of God? Why will it be complete at the sounding of the 7th trumpet?

3. Why is John told to eat the book? Why would God ask John (and Zechariah, and possibly us) to "eat" something that would make our stomachs sour?

4. Does "prophesy to many peoples, nations, tongues and kings" have any significance to us today?

5. Who are these two witnesses? Do we know their identity?

6. Where are we first told about these two witnesses? Why does John introduce them as if we should already know whom he's talking about?

7. What is happening at the 7th trumpet? What judgment takes place here? What other biblical passages can you think of that speak of this event?

COMMENTARY NOTES

Taking a break from the seven trumpet judgments, John sees an angel with great authority. This section leads us to believe that as we on earth endure the worst of all world-wide calamities we will be given prophetic insight and power. From the hidden words of the seven thunders to John's call to eat the scroll and prophesy (just like Ezekiel), to the two prophets, this section is full of a promise of divine revelation.

Amos 3:7 tells us, "Surely the Lord God does nothing, unless He reveals His secret to His servants the prophets." This section of Revelation should be understood in context of Amos 3. If biblical precedent is worth anything, the time of Revelation should be filled with the greatest outpouring of revelatory information in history. The prophet Joel reiterates this:

> 28"And it shall come to pass afterward that I will pour out My Spirit on all flesh; Your sons and your daughters shall prophesy, Your old men shall dream dreams, Your young men shall see visions.
>
> 29And also on My menservants and on My maidservants I will pour out My Spirit in those days."
>
> *Joel 2:28-29*

THE ANGEL AND THE BOOK

It is no coincidence here that the great angel John sees lets out a shout like the roar of a lion. This is representative of the prophetic ministry just as in Amos 3. When the great angel lets out his cry, the seven thunders spoke their prophetic word. It is not by accident that John heard the seven thunders. God didn't have an "oops moment" when He let John hear them that He would then immediately prohibit him from writing down what they said. This is for the people of the great tribulation to understand that there is more revelation to be given at the appropriate time.

In Daniel 8:26 we are told that the interpretation of Daniel's vision is to be sealed up because it "refers to many days in the future." All this points to God's plan to use the prophetic ministry to guide His people in the troubling end times. We will need the operative prophetic word of God in addition to a thorough understanding of Revelation to navigate the end times. These seven thunders will be revealed, as will the interpretation of the days in Daniel 8, in their proper time.

There will be many other things revealed by God to His saints through His prophets during this period. Those prophetic words, however, will never contradict what God's written Word says. The false prophet will be chief amongst those trying to lead people astray with his words and prophecies. We're even told that the false prophet will command signs in the heavens to back up his prophetic words (Deuteronomy 13:1), but that we aren't to listen to him because his words are contrary to written scripture.

The saints alive during the tribulation will have to lean heavily on God, and in this passage He is giving us confidence that He will guide us in our greatest time of need.

John is told to take the little scroll out of the angel's hand and eat it. This is identical to the situation in Ezekiel 3:1-3. Ezekiel is told to eat the scroll, which in description looks just like the scroll that Jesus took from the right hand of the Father in Revelation 5; it has writing on both sides. Both men ate the scroll of the prophetic, both were told to prophesy about the things to come, and both men said it tasted sweet in their mouth. Both were also told that it would be a hard thing for them. John's stomach turned sour after he ate it.

Ezekiel was given a warning by God that the children of Israel wouldn't listen to him because they were stubborn. This is one in the same with John's revelation here. The "bitter pill" of the end-time prophetic is that people will not listen and so be destroyed. In fact, they will cause the bearer of such news great pain. We, as John and Ezekiel, are to preach what God gives to us, without regard to how men react to it.

Before John takes the book and eats it, the angel tells us that in the days when the seventh trumpet is sounded that the mystery of the ages will be revealed. This means that prophecy will end in that day because we will be face to face with God in heaven. Paul tells us in 1 Corinthians 15:52 that at the last trumpet the rapture happens (this is the actual passage that the word "rapture" comes from). And in the days when God brings His heavenly and earthly kingdom together (eternity) Paul tells us we will see fully (1 Corinthians 13:12). We will have no need for the prophetic ministry in that day when we see God.

So, when the 7th trumpet sounds, we will see God. All the saints who have not already died will be gathered in the sky to meet Jesus, according to Paul. All those that have died will rise and meet Him there too.

If we are to gather anything from this passage, it is that in the final days before Jesus returns (in the 7th trumpet), we will have incredible prophetic power. Prophecy is coming to an end very soon, and God intends to give His favorite gift (1 Corinthians 14:1) like never before. It's going out with a bang!

THE RAPTURE

This is also a good time to say a little more about the rapture since this angel has brought up the coming seventh trumpet. The last trumpet is singled out as one of the most important events in Revelation by this angel and the heavenly chorus we'll see later.

Some have tried to say that Paul's mention of "the last trumpet" is somehow separate from the seventh trumpet of Revelation because they are already prejudiced toward believing in a "pre-tribulation" rapture. The pre-tribulation rapture has certainly been popularized today, but we must carefully look at the Bible and determine our interpretation without prejudice.

There is no coincidence with God. We have seen that He has been very intentional about giving consistent revelation to many people scattered across several hundred years. Ezekiel, Zechariah, Daniel, Jesus, Paul and John all have corroborating reports of end-time events. Why would Paul's statement of the "last trumpet" somehow be different?

The truth is that Paul is describing the very same event this giant angel is introducing us to. It is the moment to both Paul and John that we meet Jesus in the air and all the mysteries of God are revealed. We'll look at the seventh trumpet in detail in the next chapter.

One reason for reading Revelation once a week during this study is to fill our hearts and minds with God's Word. Very often our minds are prejudiced toward teaching we've received that isn't in scripture. If the idea of the rapture occurring at the seventh trumpet is new to you, study the scriptures provided here all the more carefully.

THE TEMPLE

We begin chapter 11 with John being commanded to measure the Temple. We're never told the measurements he takes, because that's not important. The important part is that the Temple exists. By the time John is writing this, the Temple in Jerusalem had already been rubble for around twenty years. It has been that way ever since 70 CE, yet we are told that it will be there, for sure. This again flows with the common theme here of the prophetic.

This has proven one of the most difficult things throughout Christian history for people to believe in Revelation. For over 1,800 years it seemed almost inconceivable that Israel would once again exist. Not believing Revelation 11:1-2 has taken the church through her history to some very dangerous conclusions and errors. For ages church leaders have believed that since there is no Israel and no Temple then the words of Revelation must be figurative. They must have meaning other than what is written on the page.

Despite God's track record of keeping His Word, men have thrown this aside and believed whatever they wanted to. The unbelief in this one verse has led to more harm in 1,900 years than is imaginable. Jews, by the millions, have been murdered because if this is just figurative then they must no longer be God's chosen people; so the thinking goes.

Israel does now, in fact, exist. It came about through no small human effort and certainly not without the miraculous hand of God. The temple being rebuilt, literally, is now the most commonly held belief here.

God's Word has proven itself accurate time and time again, so we must always be careful not to rationalize away some section of the book as figurative without a clear mandate to do so.

The angel here tells John to measure a physical temple, so we must assume from this that one will again exist. Much of what is coming in Revelation depends on it.

THE TWO PROPHETS

We've already discussed how God will reveal events in the end times that have not yet been revealed. To whom, we don't know; only that He will. The two prophets that come on the scene here will certainly be chief among the prophets of God in the Great Tribulation.

We see here that this parenthetical section covers the entirety of the Great Tribulation. We are told that these two prophets will prophesy for 42 months (3-½ years). We're told this here because the 1,260 days is about to end. The period of the great tribulation that saints will endure ends with the death and resurrection of these two, and that's why we're being told this here.

This is also the first mention of this time frame in the book of Revelation. We're not given any background information on what this 3-½ years is because we're expected to understand that this is the second half of Daniel's 70th "seven."

> *24Seventy weeks are determined for your people and for your holy city, to finish the transgression, to make an end of sins, to make reconciliation for iniq-*

*uity, to bring in everlasting righteousness, to **seal up vision and prophecy**, and to anoint the Most Holy.*

25"Know therefore and understand, that from the going forth of the command to restore and build Jerusalem until Messiah the Prince, there shall be seven weeks and sixty-two weeks; the street shall be built again, and the wall, even in troublesome times.

26"And after the sixty-two weeks Messiah shall be cut off, but not for Himself; and the people of the prince who is to come shall destroy the city and the sanctuary. The end of it shall be with a flood, and till the end of the war desolations are determined.

*27Then he shall confirm a covenant with many for **one week**; but in the **middle** of the week he shall bring an end to sacrifice and offering. and on the wing of abominations shall be one who makes desolate, even until the consummation, which is determined, is poured out on the desolate."*

*Daniel 9:24-27 (**emphasis mine**)*

"Week" can also be translated as "seven" so that the passage reads "Seventy sevens." It would be our practice today to quote the source of information we're referencing, but that wasn't always the case in John's day. Daniel's prophecy is certainly being referenced here and we must understand that to make sense of these numbers.

Again, the "two olive trees and lampstands that stand before the Lord" in 11:4 may be confusing because John speaks of this like we should know what it means, yet he hasn't spoken of this before. That's because this is a direct reference to Zechariah 4.

He does, unlike Zechariah, define what they do. They'll be calling fire down on people (from their mouths, actually), causing plagues by the words of their mouths and many other miraculous signs that won't be so well received by those who have taken the beast's mark. No one can kill them until the beast finally has his way three and a half days before the end of the 1,260 days.

The reference to "Sodom and Egypt" is Jerusalem because we are specifically told it is the city our "Lord was crucified." No one has ever heard of Jerusalem referred to as Sodom and Egypt, so this is puzzling. It could be something the Lord will reveal in time or it may be a hint that this reference is forthcoming for some reason. Right now we just don't know.

Something else we don't know is the identity of the two prophets. Some have said they must be Elijah and Enoch because neither of them experienced a natural death. That's an interesting and quite possibly a valid theory, but it is just a theory. We must be careful not to make too much of our conjecture. We're not given their identity, but it looks as though we will have no trouble recognizing whom they are when they appear.

These two will then rise to life and ascend to heaven in view of everyone. This is what starts the procession of believers into the heavens and ushers in the last 30 days or so of this "age" as we will see next.

John drops a lot of new information in this chapter. We've already seen the "last week," the "two olive trees," and now he tells us there's a beast that will ascend out of the pit. If your attention hasn't been grabbed by this book yet, it certainly should be now!

THE LAST TRUMPET

The mighty angel of Revelation 10 told us that when the seventh angel blew his trumpet, the mystery of God would be revealed. All the saints and prophets of old have been waiting for this very event. We should therefore understand that is one of the single most important events in the book.

The song that all heaven sings here in the last half of chapter 11 tells us that there's something different and something very special about what's going on here. There are only three times in Revelation that all heaven erupts into song like this: 1) When John sees the throne room, heaven responds to the presence of God and Jesus, 2) here in chapter 11 and 3) when Babylon falls in 18-19. That should be a clue that something special is happening here.

The other clue we have here is that the elders fall on their faces. They haven't done this since John saw Jesus' entry into the throne room to receive the "battle plan" (scroll). Now that battle plan is almost complete.

This is the very moment when "all eyes will see Jesus" as described in Revelation 1. This is the moment when "we'll all be changed" as Paul describes. As we'll see play out in the next few chapters, the 1,260 days comes to an end at the sounding of the 7th trumpet. This is a significant event, as the people of God have only been allotted that long to endure the tribulation.

Another clue here is that heaven is telling us that the time has come at the 7th trumpet for God to reward His servants the prophets and saints. We understand that this is when all those who have lived past and present who believe in Jesus are now standing before Him. We're told that God's temple in heaven was opened, as if it was closed before. This alludes to the veil being torn at Jesus' sacrifice during his first advent. This is an important detail as we're told in other places that those who follow Jesus will be "pillars in His Temple". We're forever given access directly to the throne of God like we've been promised.

Twice Paul references the "rapture" to the Corinthians and the Thessalonians. In the Thessalonians account he only says at "the sound of a trumpet" (4:16) will the rapture occur, but to the Corinthians (15:51) he is specific; "at the last trumpet". We have already talked about why we should understand this as corroborative revelation, not disparate trumpets as some have claimed.

Paul claims (rather coyly) in 2 Corinthians 12 that he had the same type of experience that John had; seeing the heavenly throne room. If he saw those things, why wouldn't he have access to some of the same information as John? Again, John wasn't the first person to see these things. Ezekiel, Daniel, and Zechariah, just to name a few, far predated John, so why would Paul had to have waited to hear about all this from John's book?

The reality is that Paul speaks at length about the end times in many of his epistles because he too had specific revelation about the events to come, but he apparently didn't have the same mandate as John to speak freely about it. When we hear Paul say "last trumpet" we should really pay attention. This is not a random or different trumpet, but the exact same one that John is telling us about here in chapter 11. This is, in fact, the rapture; the glorious hope of the saints past and present. This is our glorious hour where we will indeed see Jesus face to face!

Don't forget to read Revelation this week!
Visit 10WeekBible.com for more resources including daily
podcasts, videos and more.

REVELATION 12-14

STUDY QUESTIONS

1. Is Revelation meant to be literal or symbolic? If literal, how do we know when Revelation is in fact speaking symbolically?

2. Who is the woman in chapter 12? Where, specifically, might "she" be at the time of the "abomination of desolation?"

3. Who is the dragon cast down to the earth? When will he be cast down to the earth? What is meant by "earth" in this passage?

4. What are the 1,260 days? When will they happen and how will we know when they start?

5. Who is the beast? Where will he come from? What is the meaning of his "resurrection?"

6. What is the mark of the beast? Can you take it on accident? How will you know if you've taken it? What are some of the things associated with taking the mark?

7. What is Babylon? Where is it? How can we be sure that it will someday exist?

8. What is the "winepress of God's wrath?" Does this change your view of who Jesus is?

COMMENTARY NOTES

There is likely more symbolism in these three chapters than all the rest of Revelation combined. That fact often throws people off the path here. We must tackle these chapters with the mindset that Jesus is not trying to make this impossible to understand, but that like in His parables, we must have a mind to understand.

> *Therefore I speak to them in parables, because seeing they do not see, and hearing they do not hear, nor do they understand.*

> *Matthew 13:13*

That means the meaning won't always be perfectly clear, but if we study and seek Him for answers, He'll give them in time.

Most of Revelation is intended to be understood literally. This is one place where that isn't necessarily the case. We can be confident that this is a very symbolic passage because John starts by saying he saw a "sign." This is much like the horsemen John saw-they are obviously very symbolic. But the symbolism has great meaning that God wants us to search out. Let's start by listing the symbolism in these passages, along with their interpreting references:

1. WOMAN CLOTHED WITH THE SUN, MOON UNDER HER FEET & GARLAND OF 12 STARS

The woman is commonly understood as Israel, or the "remnant of Israel" (Jewish Christians) because her offspring, those who hold the testimony of Jesus (12:17) are later persecuted. Obviously the church didn't give birth to Jesus. Mary, and for the purpose of this symbol, Israel, gave birth to this male child. We must be careful not to exclude Israel from this symbol. Never forget that Jesus is still a Jewish man sitting on His Father's throne. The 12 stars reiterate that Israel is still involved as the 12 tribes of Israel.

The sun and moon symbolism has been, and still to some point remains a mystery. Rick Larson (BethlehemStar.net) has discovered some very interesting things about this, though. John says what he saw was a "sign." This usually means something in the stars or the heavens. Mr. Larson shows, very convincingly, that John was seeing an astronomical event. It's worth investigation, but the meaning is still somewhat unclear.

It's interesting to note that the woman will be protected for 1,260 days. This is another reference to the length of the Great Tribulation. This also leads us to believe that Jesus is specifically talking about Jewish Christians living in the Jerusalem area at this time.

> ¹⁵"Therefore when you see the 'abomination of desolation,' spoken of by Daniel the prophet, standing in the holy place" (whoever reads, let him understand), ¹⁶"then let those who are in Judea flee to the mountains. ¹⁷Let him who is on the housetop not go down to take anything out of his house. ¹⁸And let him who is in the field not go back to get his clothes. ¹⁹But woe to those who are pregnant and to those who are nursing babies in those days! ²⁰And pray that your flight may not be in winter or on the Sabbath. ²¹For then there will be great tribulation, such as has not been since the beginning of the world until this time, no, nor ever shall be. ²²And unless those days were shortened, no flesh would be saved; but for the elect's sake those days will be shortened.
>
> *Matthew 24:15-22*

Jesus' words in Matthew are very specific towards those living in Israel and Jerusalem specifically. We will find out later that the Antichrist will take captive Jews living in Jerusalem and here Jesus says that when the Antichrist takes over the temple as Daniel prophesied the faithful should flee. Flee where? To a place where they will be protected for 1,260 days. This again is no coincidence between biblical passages.

The "abomination of desolation" is the event that begins the last 3-½ years, or the Great Tribulation. It will happen in Jerusalem and Jesus tells the people when they see this to literally run away as fast as they can. In Revelation He promises He will protect them.

2. GAVE BIRTH TO A (MALE) CHILD WHO RULES WITH A ROD OF IRON

This is a definite reference to Jesus (Revelation 2:27, 19:15; Psalm 2:8-9) as Messiah.

3. FIERY RED DRAGON WITH 7 HEADS, 10 HORNS & 7 CROWNS

We're told explicitly in this chapter that this dragon is Satan. His heads, horns & crowns line up somewhat with the beast, but not exactly. We can understand these to mean dominions, authority and power (what heads, crowns & horns stand for biblically), but we don't know what they specifically represent. We may not until the proper time when God reveals it or it becomes apparent.

4. THIRD OF THE STARS THROWN TO EARTH

This is a reference to Satan having authority over the ⅓ of angels who sided with him in his rebellion against God. We're told of it symbolically later in this chapter as well as in Ezekiel 28.

The Bible actually says very little about Satan's origin. There's quite a bit written in Jewish literature about it and it's a well-established fact there that Satan rebelled against God and the ⅓ of the heavenly angels who sided with him were ultimately rejected by God. We can have confidence that in this case the Jewish literature is correct because the Bible treats it as such.

5. CHILD CAUGHT UP TO GOD

Again, Jesus as Messiah. This is a symbolic narrative, at this point, of the past and not the future to come.

6. 1,260 DAYS

Daniel is first told this time frame by the angel Gabriel in Daniel 12:7. This is the same as 42 months and "time, times and half a time."

It's important to note that this is according to a Jewish calendar. 1,260 days equals 3-½ years if you use twelve 30-day months per year. This is how the Jewish calendar works. In a Gregorian calendar (what we Westerners use) this period will actually be a little less than 3-½ years, but it will still be 1,260 days.

7. DRAGON CAST TO EARTH

This is commonly viewed as something that happened in the past, but we're given no inclination that is the case here. In fact, from the point of the "child being caught up to God" we're intended to understand everything in the vision as not yet happening.

Some assert that this "falling" happened at Christ's work on the cross, but again, this text leads us to believe it's happening in the same time frame as the woman fleeing and being protected during the 1,260 days.

If this is in fact a future event, it can lead us to some very sobering conclusions. "Cast to earth" could quite possibly mean that Satan and his demons would be confined to the physical realm of earth. The ancients used to refer to four realms, as quoted in the Bible. The first was earth, the second was the first heaven, or the sky. The next was the second heaven, or whatever lies beyond the clouds where the stars are. The fourth realm was the third heaven, or wherever it is that God lives.

When we view this in light of the ancients' understanding of the heavens and earth, it could mean a chilling reality of literally living with demons on earth. We'll know for sure when we get there, but it may not be such a far-fetched idea given the "wow" factor God has already employed in this book.

8. SERPENT

This is another reference to the dragon, this time with the familiar name of the serpent, the first name attributed to him in the Bible when Satan deceived Eve and Adam. This is spoken as a means of naming him as that same deceiver from the garden since he is called the serpent "of old."

9. TIME, TIMES AND HALF A TIME

This is another way of saying 3-½ years or 1,260 days; a "time" being understood as a year.

10. FLOOD OF WATER FROM SERPENT'S MOUTH & THE EARTH SWALLOWING THE FLOOD

There is nothing else in scripture that alludes to what this may mean. It could be a foreshadowing of some natural event that will take place as Israel flees the holy land for their appointed hiding place, or it could be a metaphorical "flood" of some kind. We'll definitely know when it happens and we have the dignity to ask God beforehand to explain its meaning to us in the proper time.

11. STANDING ON THE SAND OF THE SEA

There is dispute among scholars on how to translate this passage. Some translations say that John is standing on the sand of the sea while others attribute the dragon as being the one standing on the sand of the sea. There is also dispute, based on that interpretation, on whether this should be at the end of chapter 12 or the beginning of chapter 13. Keep in mind that the chapters and verses were not part of the original manuscripts, but added 1,000 years later for easy referencing of biblical passages. If you've read different translations and have noticed this, that's why.

It seems more likely that the person standing on the sand is John, since he's watching the beast arise out of the sea. We understand that the sea represents the "sea of humanity" from other passages of scripture, especially Revelation 17:15 where the angel tells John that the harlot Babylon will arise out of these "many waters."

12. BEAST WITH 7 HEADS, 10 HORNS, 10 CROWNS & BLASPHEMOUS NAME: LIKE A LEOPARD, BEAR & LION.

This is an allusion to the realms of authority that the beast will have, but we do not know now exactly what those will be. There has been great speculation as to what nations these spheres of authority will be, but they invariably fall down under the scrutiny of time.

So many nations have risen and fallen since men have tried to foresee what they were that our only realistic option is to know for certain that there will be some way in which the beast is honored by ten "heads" and ten "horns." We cannot know who or what they will be until the time that God reveals it or we see it clearly before us. Anything more than this would be an unrealistic expectation of scripture to fit our contemporary fabrications of what this means.

When these nations (we can certainly say the ten horns are nations as explained in Revelation 17:12) arise, we will certainly understand then, if the Lord has not revealed it beforehand. As of right now, He has not.

13. Mortally wounded head

This is commonly understood to mean that the beast will have died and risen again, a satanic allusion to the Christ as his offering to the world for salvation. Some have said that it may be a "political death and resurrection," but we have no way of knowing until the Lord reveals it or we see it. Again, to make up our minds beforehand would be foolish in that we may make up our minds incorrectly and then miss the real event when it actually happens.

14. 42 months

Another way of saying the 3-½ years or 1,260 days. In a long passage of so many strange and difficult metaphors, we are given this timing in three different ways so that there can be no mistake that this is yet future and very literal. The body of Christ will need to know that from the day that the "abomination of desolation" is set up, we have a very concrete number of days before Jesus will rescue us from the antichrist. This will be of great importance and of great comfort to all believers who will be counting down the days. We can confidently tell lost people not to take the mark of the beast because they will only have so many days left according to this passage.

Though we may not know the "day or the hour" of Jesus' coming before the Great Tribulation starts, once it has begun we will be able to calculate it precisely. We are told that we will certainly know when the "abomination of desolation" occurs. From that moment a clock will tick down to the triumphant reappearing of Jesus.

15. ANOTHER BEAST OUT OF THE EARTH WITH 2 HORNS LIKE A LAMB & SPEAKING LIKE A DRAGON

This is the third person of the "unholy trinity;" the dragon (Satan), the beast (the antichrist) and the other beast (the false prophet, as he is called several other times). He will look gentle, but he will be a ruthless as the first beast, the antichrist.

This "unholy trinity" is an intentional ploy by Satan to deceive the nations into thinking he is actually their god. Jesus said it would be so convincing it would "deceive even the elect, if that were possible." (Matthew 24:24)

16. MARK OF THE BEAST

Don't take it! That may be the primary message of much of the mid-section of the book of Revelation. No one who takes this mark will enter the Kingdom of God, but will suffer eternally in the lake of fire (Revelation 14:9-11).

To have "taken" the mark, there must also be an aspect of worship associated with it. It cannot be involuntarily taken; so there will be no accidents. The image of the beast must be worshipped and 14:9 makes it very clear that worship of the beast and accepting his mark go hand in hand, but it will certainly make life more difficult for those who don't take the mark; they will be forced underground since all official means of exchange will only take place if you have the mark of the beast.

Buying food will become much more difficult and it may become impossible for believers to own property, etc. Daniel 11:40-45 hints that there may be geographic regions that rebel against the control of the antichrist's system, which is great news for the saints. Isaiah 19:18-22 also hints that there may be whole regions out of his control, but we don't know that for sure.

No matter what, we must not take the mark and we must convince others not to either.

17. NUMBER OF THE BEAST: 666

Most scholars agree that this is gematria; where the number stands for a name where each letter of the name is assigned a value and added up it equals this number. For instance, the name "John" would have a numeric value of 1119 in Greek.

We don't yet know what form this mark will take. It could be a physical mark or it could be a modern implant that is read electronically. As before, to make up our minds before it happens or before the Lord speaks clearly and to many trusted prophetic voices would be foolish. We will certainly know at the right time; God is not going to let believers accidentally take this mark. That does not mean we should neglect being vigilant to watch, however.

John does give us a hint that it may take wisdom to discern what this mark truly is; meaning we will definitely want to devote energy to understanding this beforehand. This discernment needs to come mainly in the form of seeking prophetic revelation from God. When a large number of trusted prophetic voices have consensus that affirms scripture, we may have confidence in this mark then; but not before. Anything else would be chasing straw men.

18. The 144,000 who lead in song

Some have equated this group with the 144,000 from the 12 tribes of Israel. As with many other things, God doesn't create coincidences, but He doesn't specifically say they are the same.

Either way, this group is going to be a literal group of male leaders who have remained virgin. Why that's important we're not told, only that they are. This group harkens back to David's leadership of his tabernacle listed in 1 Chronicles 25 (although David's list had 288 leaders, or two times 144 to cover 24 hours a day).

19. Babylon

The book of Revelation spends more time speaking about Babylon than any other single subject. This is because Babylon is the main reason for the last days. Revelation chapters 17-19:5 is all about Babylon's fall and a description of the things Babylon did. Babylon is the coming world-wide system that will be horrendously oppressive to Jews and Christians. The world has never faced an evil like this before and it is the reason that God is going to pour out His wrath on the earth.

There is a world system aspect to Babylon, but it is also clear that Babylon will literally be the city of Babylon. The angel tells John that Babylon is "that great city which reigns over the kings of the earth" in Revelation 17:18.

Babylon the city does not now exist, which has caused some scholars to rationalize away Babylon as some other city, like New York or Rome, or to say that it is not a city at all. But this is simply not having faith in scripture. For thousands of years the prevailing eschatology was that Revelation is completely figurative because there was no nation of Israel and no one could conceive of there ever being a nation of Israel again. That idea came crashing down almost "overnight" as after nearly 1,800 years Israel came into existence.

The same is true with Babylon. Although it still lies in ruin, it will certainly rise from its ashes, to the shame of the world. Cities like Dubai, UAE give us a precedent for just how quickly one of the greatest cities on earth can rise from the sand. But like so many other things that haven't happened yet, we must not be too convinced of something except that we trust that scripture is correct. One thing is for certain though: Babylon will surely rise again.

20. HARVESTING THE EARTH

This is a metaphor that harkens back to Jesus' words on the end times in Matthew 13 when he explains the parable of the wheat and tares to His disciples. Jesus has waited for the end of the age for the tares, the wicked, to grow up into their full wickedness before He punishes them. Likewise, He has also waited until the end of the age to harvest the righteous so that their works may be "perfect in the sight of His God."

21. WINEPRESS OF GOD'S WRATH

This is another metaphor, this time where the flow of grape juice out of a winepress represents the blood of those being executed in the judgments of the Lord. Jesus is literally going to execute those who have taken the mark of the beast and kill them outside Jerusalem so that in places their blood will flow like a river as high as a horse's bridle (4-5 feet) for several hundred miles.

That's a lot of execution and it's offensive to many that Jesus Himself would do this. Many have falsely attributed weakness to Jesus, in that He doesn't "have it in Him" to do such a thing, but we must remember that He is fully God as well as fully man. He will be the physical man who exacts judgment on the wicked of the earth in the last days. Jesus is not a little porcelain baby lying in a manger, nor is He just a suffering servant hanging on a cross. He is a conquering warrior who will avenge His name and His people from the world that has grown horribly wicked in the last days.

We will see in the coming chapters just how bad the world will become before Jesus' return. If we miss that fact, Revelation will be hard to make sense of. We must know that as the end times come upon us, there will be an increase in wickedness that the world has never seen before.

So that's a lot of symbolism to understand! It's not intended to be easy, but it is intended to be understood. Don't let the difficulty persuade you to think that Jesus is trying to make it impossible; He's not. He's just trying to force us to study it out, speak with Him about it and trust His leading in understanding over time.

Don't forget to read Revelation this week!
Visit 10WeekBible.com for more resources including daily
podcasts, videos and more.

REVELATION 15-16

STUDY QUESTIONS

1. What is the sea of glass? Why might it be "mingled with fire?"

2. Why would heaven sing the song of Moses and the Lamb? Why wouldn't God write His own songs to be sung on such an occasion?

3. Why do you think God would seal Himself inside the temple for the seven bowls?

4. What are the differences between the bowl judgments and the seals and trumpets? Why are the bowl judgments so different?

5. Why does the angel who releases the third bowl proclaim God just in His action? What are the implications of the third bowl?

6. What is destroyed in the earthquake of bowl seven? What else is included in the seventh bowl that's particularly angering to the inhabitants of earth? What would this kind of plague do to buildings, roads, bridges, etc.?

7. Why would John keep introducing things in the book that require us to read further to understand? How should that alter the way we read Revelation?

COMMENTARY NOTES

John wastes no time in chapter 15 telling us that we're about to experience the end of God's battle plan to rid the earth of the wicked. There are seven more angels who are going to carry out God's wrath standing up preparing themselves to carry out their duty.

ANTICIPATION

Also in attendance at this event is the host of heavenly saints waiting in anticipation for Jesus to carry out His vengeance He promised in Seal 5. We are told plainly that this sea of glass, represented in the Temple days by the sea that stood in the courtyard, is the innumerable throng of saints. This time the sea of saints are mixed with fire. We don't know exactly what this means, but it sounds a lot like they are consumed by the same fiery zeal of God He spoke of in Song of Solomon:

> "Set me as a seal upon your heart, as a seal upon your arm; for love is as strong as death, jealousy as cruel as the grave; its flames are flames of fire, a most vehement flame."
>
> Song of Solomon 8:6

God has given all the saints harps with which to sing a song attributed to Moses and Jesus. They are called the harps of God. This brings up an interesting allusion. When David was preparing Solomon to build the temple, he made special note that all the instruments prepared for the 24/7 worship were made by him (1 Chronicles 23:5). He seems to take unusual pride in the instruments.

David never comes out and says it, but we have good reason to believe that he saw what John saw here. When he gives Solomon the plans for the temple, he said,

"All this," said David, "the Lord made me understand in writing, by His hand upon me, all the works of these plans."

1 Chronicles 28:19

It's interesting to note that God has made such a big deal of worship throughout scripture. We may take it for granted, but here we see that it's not only the duty and privilege of every person to worship God, but also to participate in the leading of that worship. There are two main worship movements outlined in scripture; David's and this one here before God's throne. David's went on around the clock 24/7 and we see in Revelation 4:8 that this one does too.

This should cause us to pause for a moment and consider our lives now. If God used David to establish a worship movement based upon the heavenly model to be used on earth, what does that compel us to do today? Amos prophesied that in the last days God would raise up "David's fallen tent" as a reference to David's 24/7 worship movement (Amos 9:11). This knowledge should cause us to examine our time and energy as a church and personally. How do we reflect God's model in heaven and that which He's promised to raise up on earth?

SONG OF MOSES

Whereas there is no direct quote of Moses in this song of "Moses and the Lamb," it seems to be a version of Deuteronomy 32:3-4. It could be that this is the version co-written by Jesus and Moses? If that seems far-fetched for

God to collaborate with his creation, consider all the promises Jesus gives us in chapters 2-3 of sharing His rulership with us. Also consider the fact that on the mount of transfiguration Jesus conferred with Moses and Elijah (Luke 9:28-36).

This chapter is a beautiful promise to the saints who have just suffered under intense persecution at the hands of the wicked on earth. The saints in this "sea mixed with fire" are being included in this final phase of God's battle plan on earth. Whereas the saints' prayers seem to be part of what releases the seals and trumpets, as we've already discussed, it's evident here that the saints are now an integral part of the bowls of wrath.

This level of partnership with God should cause us to consider ourselves carefully. The dignity, honor and eternal value God has ascribed to those who have accepted His son are nearly unimaginable. How that we, a rebellious people justly deserving the same wrath being poured out on the earth, are not only spared that fate but offered eternal glory is certainly the most magnificent mystery of all eternity.

JUDGMENT

Some people struggle with the concept here in this song (and in Revelation in general) of God's judgment. The word judgment has been somewhat perverted in our Western culture. Judgment here certainly has a negative connotation towards those who are being judged, but we often feel as though it's wrong to judge. We must consider what is taking place. In a court of law, an offended party is asking for judgment against an adversary. Be it a thief, a murderer or someone who has defrauded us, we want justice to be served.

God is exacting this same kind of justice in Revelation. His judgments are "just and true" as the song says. Jesus is the only one worthy to make these judgments upon the earth because even the righteous saints are only made righteous through the shed blood of Jesus. So we need not be put off by the thought of judgment in Revelation because it is God standing up for Himself and for us to avenge all the evil that has been done against us. He is our righteous judge handing down justice from the high court of heaven.

ANGELS DRESSED IN WHITE

Out of the temple come angels dressed in the same garb as Jesus is described in chapter 1: white clothes with a golden sash. This is intriguing as to the order of heaven God has ordained. These seven special angels must have some high place as they seem to have been locked up in the temple in heaven until this very time. That they are the only other beings in heaven dressed as Jesus is also interesting.

At this point God "locks" Himself inside the temple so that no one can come in or see Him while He exacts His final judgments on the earth. We haven't been privy to all the activities of heaven through time, but this is certainly the only time in scripture where God obscures Himself from everyone. Just like the 30 minutes of silence before the trumpet judgments, God is declaring a holy moment here.

FIRST BOWL

As the bowls begin we immediately see that these are different than seals and trumpets. No longer affecting ¼ or ⅓ of earth, these exact total destruction as they are carried out.

Sores are poured out only on those that have taken the mark of the beast in the first bowl. This brings up an interesting point. If all God's people have been raptured at this point, who is left but those who took the mark? There will be three groups of people throughout the Great Tribulation: 1) the saints, 2) those allied with the beast and 3) resistors.

This third group we will later find out will be the small few who will alone survive Jesus' final judgment carried out at Jerusalem. They will enter the millennial kingdom and are not the recipients of any of these bowl judgments.

Many people view the conflict in Revelation as somehow more-than-human because of the supernatural nature of the judgments, but in fact the Antichrist's reign is very human. We see in Daniel 11 that he will be fighting wars from rebelling nations all throughout the Great Tribulation. His rule will not be universal, but it will be far more universal than any ruler in history. This means that like any military conflict throughout the ages there will be people who neither ally themselves with Jesus and the saints but neither will they take the mark of the beast and ally themselves with the Antichrist. These resisters will not be affected by several of the bowls.

As the second bowl begins we get the impression that these are moving very rapidly. There is good reason to believe that all seven bowls are occurring within a 30-day time frame. We'll discuss that a little later.

SECOND BOWL

The sea is again touched by a plague of blood, but this time it's complete. Now everything in the sea is dead. If anyone's way of life depended on the sea, it's now over.

If goods are still being shipped by sea at this point, I can't begin to imagine how unpleasant life would be for any mariners unfortunate enough to travel the seas. The stench from billions and billions of rotting fish would be unbearable.

THIRD BOWL

Man can live without salt water, but not without fresh water. It's unclear here how anyone would survive longer than a few days if this is in fact total disruption of the fresh water supply. Rivers and springs certainly means surface and ground water, where all our drinking water comes from. Maybe stores of treated water won't be touched, but that would account for such a small fraction of people's basic needs. All the water towers on earth can't hold enough water to keep even who are left alive going.

This is such a merciless and onerous judgment that the angel who pours it out feels the need to proclaim the authority of God to even carry out such a thing. He makes it clear that this is God's retribution to those on earth for their hand in shedding His people's blood. A voice from the altar agrees with the angel and reiterates that God is just in this.

As if the lives of those left alive weren't already miserable enough, this is indeed a devastating catastrophe. This may be the worst plague to befall the earth yet, but more is to come.

FOURTH BOWL

Now the sun turns on the people of earth and they know who is doing it to them. The people do not repent and glorify God but instead blaspheme His name. This is what these judgments are all about. God is revealing the true nature of sin and the heart of man.

Even when they know God is at work and they understand He is acting against them, they still choose to shake their fists at Him. The people of earth have joined Satan in his total rebellion against God.

FIFTH BOWL

Like the seal and trumpet series, the first three bowls share a similar theme of some kind of physical judgment. Starting with the fifth bowl, God moves in a different direction. Like in Egypt, God casts the wicked into darkness.

This may not seem like a judgment at first, but imagine what it must be like now. These people are in constant pain from the sores they acquired in the first bowl, but people are very good at distracting themselves from pain. By now they have probably found ways of coping with their agony.

Total darkness, the supernatural kind Egypt experienced, brings everything to a stop. Now no one can distract themselves from the pain and all their attention is on their misery. Their hearts are revealed yet again and they curse the God who breathed life into them in the first place.

SIXTH BOWL

Much like the fifth seal, this bowl is a prelude to something much worse. God actually makes it easy for the armies of the Antichrist to assemble on the east side of the Euphrates.

The "unholy trinity" of the Beast (Antichrist), False Prophet and Satan release proxy demonic spirits to muster the troops to the place universally known for the end of time: Armageddon. It should be noted that no battle actually takes place at Armageddon; this is a common misunderstanding of Revelation.

Read it carefully and you will see there is no battle here. Armageddon is the Antichrist's staging place for the world's armies to assemble before their final assault on Jerusalem. Armageddon is a large, flat valley where it will be easy for all these armies to congregate and plan their assault on Jerusalem.

The Antichrist seems to have had power over Jerusalem for the time of the Great Tribulation, so the question arises of why he would attack it in the first place. We won't get an answer to that until chapter 19, but it is worth noting that some interesting things might have been taking place.

Daniel 11:40-45 tells us that the Antichrist will be busy trying to crush rebellion against him all throughout the end times. Specifically, we're told that near the end he'll completely subdue Egypt, which must have rebelled against him. After subduing Egypt he'll rush off to the "east and the north" to destroy rebellious armies.

Daniel 11:45 tells us he will "plant the tents of his palace between the seas and the glorious holy mountain." This sounds a lot like the area of Armageddon, if the "seas" here are the Mediterranean and the Sea of Galilee.

By understanding Revelation and Daniel together we get a fuller picture of why the Antichrist is coming back to Israel from the east and why he assembles in Armageddon.

We'll have to wait to find out why he's going to attack Jerusalem, though.

SEVENTH BOWL

There's no break here like with the seals and trumpets; we jump straight to the last bowl. This is of course the worst thing to happen to planet earth yet. An earthquake worse than anything the earth has ever seen before rocks the planet and all the cities of earth "fall." Judging by the context here, fall should probably be interpreted as to literally collapse.

We're told that Babylon will succumb to the wrath of God. This is another time that John has referenced something we don't know anything about again. We don't yet know why Babylon of all the cities on earth demands the direct attention of God to be destroyed. This happens so often it's as if John is assuming we'll have already read Revelation.

Like so many books of the Bible, we must study them, read and re-read them to get them into our hearts. John makes it clear from the outset in chapter one that we must "keep" the words listed in this book. That requires us to study over and over the words of this book.

We'll find out more about Babylon soon enough now, though, as the next several chapters are dedicated to her. For now, we'll trust that Babylon is deserving of God's wrath.

One interesting thing about this last plague is that even though the greatest earthquake in human history has destroyed what was left of human infrastructure, it is not what angers the rebellious here. What makes them angry enough to blaspheme God again is a hail storm, and what a hail storm it is.

We don't know if this hail storm is centralized in one area or over a large portion of the earth, but we do know that nothing like this has ever happened before. A talent is equal to about 100 pounds. To put this in perspective, the largest hailstone ever recorded was between 6 and 8 inches in diameter. A one hundred pound hailstone would be about the size of a large couch (hailstones are rarely solid or spherical when they're large).

Don't forget to read Revelation this week!
Visit 10WeekBible.com for more resources including daily podcasts, videos and more.

REVELATION 17-19:5

1. Who is the harlot? How do we know? Is she literal or figurative?

2. Why does the angel tell us it will take "wisdom" to understand who the harlot and beast are? What is the wisdom the angel is talking about?

3. What are the seven heads of the beast? What are the 10 horns? Why does God use such strange language to describe something instead of plainly telling us?

4. What are the things that have made Babylon great? Do any of the things in that list seem strange to you?

5. Why would God's people need to come out of Babylon? Why would they have been there in the first place?

6. Why do the merchants of the earth mourn over Babylon? Is Babylon a real city?

7. Why is all the blood of the prophets and saints found in Babylon?

8. Why do you think the smoke of Babylon will rise forever and ever?

COMMENTARY NOTES

We start chapter 17 with a strange command. One of the seven angels with the bowls tells John to come so he can see the "great harlot who sits on many waters." Chapters 15-16 had presumably little symbolism, but here we seem to be jumping right back into it.

THE MYSTERY

We understand that we're speaking figuratively now because even if a woman could fornicate with the kings of the earth, no one can "drink the wine of her fornication." The phrase harlot is used many times in scripture to symbolize a people (mostly Israel) who have turned their backs on God and resorted to worshipping idols.

John is shown this woman clothed in red sitting on a red beast. She is very expensively clothed and she is holding a cup full of the figurative wickedness she embodies.

The fact that this harlot has the word "mystery" stamped on her forehead along with the other proclamations she apparently wears tells us this is not a straightforward affair. What is straightforward is that whatever she represents, it's the single-greatest threat to God's saints.

"Drunk with the blood of the martyrs of Jesus" is a chilling statement. And if you're starting to be confused by her and what she means, you're not alone. John tells us he was just as lost when he saw her too.

Fortunately for us, the "mystery" that is this woman is going to be explained.

THE BEAST

He starts by telling us who this beast is that she rides. "Was, and is not, and will ascend out of the bottomless pit" is most often thought to mean that the beast will have died and risen again. As part of Satan's plan to create an "unholy trinity" this works well. Satan needed a Messiah figure and got him with this beast.

Many have theorized that this resurrection is political or figurative in reality. Whereas these are interesting theories, and since we're speaking metaphorically about a beast anyway, we have to conclude that they are just theories. Right now, we just don't know what this will mean and since it will bring such intrigue to the world, we would be wise to leave it open for now.

What we can be sure of is that by the time he arrives the saints will not be surprised or intrigued by him or this resurrection feat. The angel promises John that those whose names are in the Book of Life will not marvel at him. As with God's promise to speak prophetically to us, we will certainly not be taken by surprise by this beast.

This beast is the Antichrist or the "man of sin" as Paul called him (2 Thessalonians 2:3). He's referred to as the beast in Revelation to describe his (and his government's) treatment of people and specifically Israel, but all the names in scripture point to this man.

SEVEN HEADS

The seven mountains that are represented by the heads have taken on many theories over time. Rome was founded on 7 hills, so it is often thought to be what this is talking about. Others believe the 7 hills are symbolic of 7 spheres of influence in society. There are so many theories, in fact, you could keep busy for weeks finding them all. Again, we don't know what these mountains are. We do know that there is a governmental component to these heads.

There will be seven world leaders over time. Similar to the vision in Daniel 10-11, John is told of world leaders through time. By the time of his writing, five of the leaders (associated with this beast) had already fallen, one was in existence at that time and one was yet to come still before the beast himself.

The most common interpretation for this is the world empires who oppressed Israel. Those that had fallen would have been Egypt, Assyria, Babylon, Persia and Greece. Rome would have been the one that was around during John's day. We're also told in Daniel 9:26-27 that the "people of the prince" who cut off the Messiah in week 69 would return in the 70th week. This leads many to believe that Rome will rise again as the precursor to this 8th king, the beast himself.

Of course we're told that to understand all this we need a mind with wisdom, just like we do to understand the mark of the beast. That wisdom can only come through prophetic revelation from God, so we must lean into Him for understanding in the day that we need it. We always, however, have the dignity to ask now. The worst God can say is "not yet."

Whereas the kingdoms of the past seem pretty clear and seem to line up with Daniel's message, we don't yet understand what that holds for the future of the 7th king and the beast. Wild speculation has abounded throughout history from every detestable ruler to the Pope being the 7th king or the beast. This is mostly unhelpful.

Keep in mind that a "mind with wisdom" does not mean a smart person. If such person existed, surely we would have figured this out after 1,900 years. No, this means revelation from God. Just as Joseph told Pharaoh that interpretations belonged to God, so do the meanings of these things. We would do better to ask God what they mean than to speculate. He will certainly reveal all in the proper time.

TEN HORNS

Again we're faced with more symbolism speaking of rulers. This time the ten horns will be contemporaries to the beast, not past world rulers. Who they are, we don't know. Again, speculation abounds, but we must refrain from that.

What we should focus on is that God has granted these ten kings plus the beast the authority to persecute and kill we Christians. This is not good news for us. In fact, this is one of the first pieces of bad news aimed directly at God's people in Revelation. But like a good Father, God has told us ahead of time of the challenges we will face.

This time will be much like the time of Israel's exodus from Egypt. The plagues were not meant for Israel, but for the Egyptians, but Israel's trouble came at the hand of Pharaoh, enraged ever more by each passing judgment. So we too will be hated and hunted by the Antichrist and his followers

BACK TO THE HARLOT

Waters, we're told here, represent the "sea of humanity," as we would likely say. This is actually a common theme used throughout Revelation. This means that the harlot is among all peoples in some form or fashion. But we're also told very bluntly that the harlot is the city Babylon. That's a hint again that there's more to this mystery than meets the eye. There must be some "both and" relationship between the future city of Babylon and a worldwide system that encompasses the wickedness described by this harlot.

Whatever the case, the beast and his kingdoms will not get along with the harlot and they will eventually decide to kill her. That probably means that they will carry out the destruction of Babylon themselves, but it could also mean a coup of her worldwide system as well.

WHAT IS BABYLON?

What we do know for sure is that Babylon, in whatever form she takes, is going to be horrendously evil. In fact, chapter 18 is a full description of her sins.

There's not much to interpret when it comes to chapter 18. This is the most straightforward part of Revelation. It is a description of the city and what it provided to the inhabitants of earth. What is worth interpretation is why so many words have been spent to describe her in this relatively short book.

This is where we begin to see the larger picture of Revelation. We are now beginning to understand the "why" behind all this. Why does God need to carry out such merciless judgments on the earth? The answer we're given is here in these passages: Babylon.

Someone in heaven proclaims that the saints must come out of Babylon at some point. Presumably God's people would be there just like any other city on earth pleading with its inhabitants to turn to God, but there's coming a day when it's too late. Just like God sparing Lot and his daughters from Sodom's fate, God will call His people out of Babylon once and for all.

Many have speculated that the description of Babylon's fall may be a nuclear explosion. This may be true, but it is just speculation. Somehow, her destruction will be unlike any other city. Either the way she is destroyed or the level of splendor that is destroyed will cause many great heartache.

The interesting thing is the level of defiance that exists in Babylon. Verse 7 tells us that she believes she "will not see sorrow." This is directly defiant to God's Word given Babylon's actions. God is going to swiftly and totally judge this spirit.

BABYLON'S INDUSTRY

The list of what is traded in Babylon is chilling. Verses 12-13 contains many of the things you would think a great trading city would have but it ends with "and bodies and souls of men." That means that not only will slavery once again rise, but in Babylon it will be done out in the open. Right now there are more people enslaved than ever before in history. Sex slaves and the sex trade is the second-largest illicit crime in the world and given all the references to the sexual insanity in Revelation it would be hard to believe this is anything else.

We are told here in chapter 18 that Babylon is going to be like nothing the world has ever seen. Everything that puts itself against the knowledge of God finds a home here. Everything evil, sinful, detestable and rebellious will be carried out with impunity in Babylon until God judges her.

BABYLON'S GREATEST SIN

Probably the most damning thing against Babylon is the last line of chapter 18; "And in her was found the blood of prophets and saints, and all who were slain on the earth." God seems to attribute all murder and martyrdom to Babylon. It seems unlikely that every person killed will be brought to Babylon to face their execution, so it seems likely that this is a hint that Babylon itself will exert quite a bit of control over the governments and laws of nations when it comes to killing the saints. This is one reason many believe Babylon will be both a literal city and a system of control.

HEAVEN REJOICES OVER BABYLON'S DESTRUCTION

Our attention is drawn to just how bad Babylon is by what takes place in chapter 19. Any time all heaven erupts into song in Revelation, we should pay very careful attention. Here all heaven rejoices over the destruction of Babylon. Again, God's righteous judgments are proclaimed as we learn that Babylon had it coming. Somehow God will cause Babylon's "smoke to rise up forever and ever."

Either literally or figuratively, it seems we will never forget Babylon's judgment for all eternity. Nothing of the same is said for Satan, the false prophet or the Antichrist. What we should take away from this is that nothing in all history has equaled the evil that will come with this city. If we are to take this literally, then something so wicked and oppressive is coming before the end times that God's saints will cry out to Him for all the plagues that we have seen preceding this.

This is the "why" of Revelation. Jesus told us in Matthew 24:24 that such great deception is coming it would deceive the saints if it were possible. We can't take this too lightly. If we are to believe Revelation, we must know that things are going to get much, much worse before Jesus returns. They will get worse before even the Great Tribulation begins. The evil attributed to Babylon will certainly take more than 3-½ years to build up.

NOT HERE...YET

One final note is that many have tried to make Babylon completely figurative. Whereas it seems Babylon is at least partially figurative, just because it doesn't currently exist doesn't mean it won't. We have some stunning examples of cities that have risen from nothing in a little more than a decade. Shanghai, China and Dubai, UAE are two examples of the power of wealth and human ingenuity to raise a city from the dust.

Don't forget to read Revelation this week!
Visit 10WeekBible.com for more resources including daily podcasts, videos and more.

REVELATION 19:6-22

STUDY QUESTIONS

1. Who does Jesus ride back to earth with? Where does He go when He comes back?

2. How does Jesus conquer the Antichrist's army? What is done with him?

3. Why will Satan be released after 1,000 years? What will happen after he is?

4. Who will be reigning on earth for 1,000 years? Who is left alive to inhabit the earth if all those who took the mark of the beast were executed?

5. How many good deeds must you do to get into heaven? What book is our eternal future judged by? What must we do to get into that book?

6. Is the eternal Jerusalem literal or figurative? How do we know that? How big could you imagine your eternal "home" to be in this city?

7. What will we eat and drink in eternity? Why is this important as we consider the story of the Bible from beginning to end?

COMMENTARY NOTES

The beginning of chapter 19 concluded the exposition on how bad Babylon was and transitioned to the saints being invited to the "marriage supper of the Lamb." This bridal language has been used many places in scripture; most famously in Song of Solomon.

God treats those as His treasured bride who have accepted His son, Jesus. At the end of time there is this "marriage" that is going to happen where we as His people are invited to. We will see from here to the end of the book that this marriage involves God bringing heaven down to earth to live with men forever.

This is a common misconception about Revelation. We will not go to heaven to spend eternity with God, but He is bringing heaven to earth forever. We will live ON EARTH forever. This couldn't be clearer in Revelation, but most believers think about eternity as some boring ride in the clouds. Thankfully, that's not the case. We will get the smallest glimpse into our eternal state from here out, but the struggle isn't quite over yet.

OUR PLACE IN HEAVEN

John has been led around by angels throughout this whole process and when he sees this marriage supper invitation he can't contain himself anymore. He falls to the ground to worship the angel and receives a quick rebuke. The angel tells John that he's not to be worshipped because they are both fellow servants of Jesus, the only object of our worship.

This is a very interesting point. Paul tells us that it was always God's intent to reveal to the heavenly creatures His mystery and wisdom through us!

> *[10]His intent was that now, through the church, the manifold wisdom of God should be made known to the rulers and authorities in the heavenly realms, [11]according to his eternal purpose which he accomplished in Christ Jesus our Lord.*
>
> *Ephesians 3:10-11 (NIV 84)*

This means that we truly are in partnership in every way with not only these angels but God as well. What an amazing journey God has invited us on. We get to partake in revealing and understanding the mystery of God not only in this world but also in heaven. We must truly be special to God!

JESUS ON A WHITE HORSE

Jesus rides in on His white horse now and we see his robes dipped in blood. Some have interpreted this as the blood Jesus shed for us but end-times scripture gives us a different perspective.

When we piece together scripture about Jesus' physical return to earth, we find that He travels around the Middle East before entering Jerusalem to war with the Antichrist's armies.

Isaiah 63:1 tells us Jesus is coming up from Edom with His robes stained in blood. Daniel told us that the Antichrist will not have control over Edom (the land on the southeast side of the Dead Sea) and that it is a likely place the people of Jerusalem and Judea will flee to on foot on the day the Antichrist sets up the "abomination of desolation."

There are other references to the Messiah visiting places immediately before entering Jerusalem we won't discuss here, but it seems like Jesus' vengeance on the part of His people has already started as He moves toward Jerusalem. He seems to gather those He's protected during the Great Tribulation (Revelation 12:6) and kills people along the way as He moves west from Edom.

The armies of heaven are clothed in white, which we understand to be the saints following Jesus. He is going to "tread the winepress of the fierceness and wrath of Almighty God." We will find out shortly that this means Jesus is literally going to kill untold scores of people as He judges from Jerusalem.

NAME ABOVE EVERY NAME

We see that Jesus' Word, the sword that comes from His mouth, is what will strike the nations. He will judge with the very Words of God. We see here His eternal title, "King of Kings and Lord of Lords." Jesus is not simply some sissy do-gooder that seems to be the picture of Him today, but the rightful ruler of heaven and earth. Paul tells us in Romans 11:22 that we should "consider the kindness and severity of God." We see here that Jesus will be kind to those who have followed and obeyed and severe to those who have rebelled.

We must not confuse rebellion with weakness, however. Many have been fearful of Revelation and meeting this vengeful God. For the redeemed, those who have accepted Jesus, we needn't fear God's wrath or His judgments. Jesus' work on the cross has born that wrath for us. For those who refuse to accept Jesus, they must bear that wrath alone. Our sin is not equal to these people's rebellion. Our weakness and sin has been covered by the cross.

THE FEAST OF GOD

We transition to what an angel calls the "feast of the great God." This is remarkably different from the wedding supper of the Lamb as mentioned before. Here we're not talking about a feast for the saints, but a morbid feast for the vultures and other carrion-eating birds. This is a forewarning of possibly the greatest single death-toll ever to take place.

Jesus is about to hand out death-sentences to millions from His new throne in Jerusalem. First of all, however, are the beast and false prophet. Jesus is going to throw them alive into the lake of fire, that eternal punishment reserved for the rebellious who refuse to accept Jesus.

I have contemplated this at length. How bad do you have to be to spend 1,000 years in hell before Satan? The lake of fire, as best we can tell from scripture, will have only two inhabitants for 1,000 years while Satan is bound and Jesus reigns on earth before the final White Throne Judgment to come. The beast and the false prophet will exist alone in the lake of fire; their stay will be eternity to come plus 1,000 years.

THE MILLENNIUM

That brings us to chapter 20 and the millennial reign of Jesus. This is the most-disputed chapter of Revelation. This is in fact where the three main diverging views of Revelation come from.

"Postmillennialism" is the term referring to people who believe that Jesus will actually return to earth after this 1,000 years. Most postmillennial scholars hold that the 1,000 years is figurative and meant to represent a time where the earth is purified by the church.

"Amillennialism" is a term used by people who believe that all Revelation is figurative and there is no definitive 1,000 years to come or that will happen at all. Revelation is simply an allegorical book meant to teach us principles God has for us.

"Premillennialism" is the term referring to people who hold that Jesus will return before the 1,000 years. This is held by those who take a more literal view of the book and is also the view held by this commentary.

If we look at Revelation 19 coming chronologically before Revelation 20, then this makes the most sense. Almost all scholars who view Revelation as prophetic scripture (something to take place in the future) view this as a literal 1,000 years that Jesus will reign on earth from Jerusalem.

THE MILLENNIUM IS UNIQUE

This 1,000 years will be different from eternity because the earth will continue on as it has since the time Adam fell with the exception that Jesus will be back on earth as it's rightful King. People will still be born and die; accept Jesus and sin and rebel during this time. Those "resisters" we discussed earlier will be earth's inhabitants. They would not have been killed for taking the mark of the beast when Jesus returned to Jerusalem.

Jesus is going to invite the saints to reign with Him during this 1,000 years. It's somewhat unclear if all saints or just the saints from the Great Tribulation (those who didn't take the mark of the beast) will be those given authority during this time. All saints will at this time have been given their glorified eternal bodies as Jesus also has, but who exactly is reigning on earth is not clear. Either way, no saint whose faith was in Jesus will suffer the "second death" to come.

After 1,000 years, Satan will be released from the prison he's been held in to deceive the nations once again. This is very puzzling to many people as to why God would release Satan only to lead people astray, but God's motives are revealed by the results.

All men throughout history have had to believe in God without seeing Him. For 1,000 years men have lived under the direct rulership of Jesus on earth. Satan is going to be released to reveal men's hearts. Given the opportunity, man will willingly rebel against the same God they saw judge the earth and put it back together over 1,000 years. These people who have lived during the millennium will be afforded the same opportunity to rebel as all men throughout history have and many will take it.

THE MILLENNIUM IN SCRIPTURE

Revelation only mentions the 1,000 year reign of Christ in passing, but scripture has much to say about this time. The Old Testament prophets are full of references to this time period. Isaiah prophesied that during this time people would begin living very long again like in the days before Noah.

> ...He who dies at a hundred will be thought a mere youth; he who fails to reach a hundred will be considered accursed.

Isaiah 65:20

Things will begin to go back to how they were shortly after the fall as Jesus restores the heavenly order to earth. Then Satan will be released for a "little while." In this little while he will lead a rebellion that will span the globe. The group will try to descend on Jerusalem where Jesus is to crush Him but God the Father will put a quick and decisive end to this. No plagues of Revelation all over again; this time the fire that will consume them for eternity will snuff their lives out before their plot ever takes shape.

All those who ally themselves with Satan at this point will have their allegiance as their witness against them. God will immediately cast them all into the lake of fire where the beast and false prophet have been. Then God will open the book of life and all whose names aren't written there will be cast into the lake of fire as well. This is only those who have not willingly decided to follow Jesus. No amount of good works as recorded in the other books will matter. All that matters is if your name is in the Book of Life.

ALL THINGS MADE NEW

The meaning of a new heaven and new earth in chapter 21 is debated between scholars. There are sufficient biblical texts to support either position. Some say the earth will not be destroyed by God's fire but only "renewed." Others say this passage means what it says. Regardless of how this takes place, things will be very different. We will live forever in a world with no sea and no sun.

God is going to wipe away all our tears. Whatever suffering and pain, sin and regret we had in this life will be taken away as we enter eternity with our maker. This is all believers' great hope. As Paul says, if Jesus wasn't raised from the dead, we are of all men most to be pitied (1 Corinthians 15:19). But if Jesus was raised from the dead, this is our eternal hope of glory; to be with God forever!

THE ETERNAL CITY JERUSALEM

Many people struggle with this city as it is described here. This city has a footprint of 1,400-1,500 miles per side and it's as tall as it is wide. It's a giant cube. To put that in perspective, the International Space Station orbits at 205 miles above the earth. This city's penthouse would be 7 times that high!

This shouldn't concern us, though. Just because we can't fathom a single city that size, we must think of its creator. He's the same one who with a word created the entire universe. The Man who created Jupiter should have no problem with this city.

What is interesting about this city is that Jesus Himself told us that He left us to go and prepare it for us. That means for almost 2,000 years now Jesus has been working on this our eternal rest. What is even more amazing is that He said it was better that He did that than to be physically with us (John 16:7). What does that mean about the splendor of this city?

John's given the tour of the city and the angel seems to make the point that this place is literal and physical. John is told to measure it with a measuring stick of heaven that coincidentally happens to be the same units that man uses. The city will be glorious as it's light is none other than God the Father and Jesus themselves. As it turns out, Jesus wasn't being "cute" when He said, "I am the light of the world." (John 8:12)

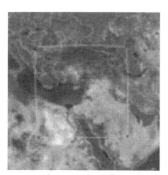

Eternal Jerusalem footprint
if centered on modern
Jerusalem

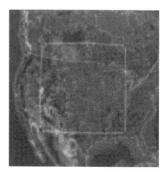

Eternal Jerusalem footprint
for reference over US &
Canada

ENDING AS WE STARTED

What is amazing about Revelation 22 is that God tells us eternity will go back to how time started in the garden. We are going to be given access to this river of the water of life and to the tree of life.

In Genesis, Adam and Eve were not forbidden from eating of the tree of life, but of the tree "of the knowledge of good and evil." (Genesis 2:17) In fact, they had to eat of the tree of life to keep living. When they were cast out of the garden for their sin it was so they could not continue eating of the tree of life. (Genesis 3:22)

We will again eat of this tree and live forever. No longer will our bodies rot from the curse Adam bestowed upon us for his sin, but we will never again taste death.

WARNING

Jesus tells John that anyone who adds or takes away from "this book" will be cursed. The book He's referring to is Revelation, not the entire Bible as some have said. While I'm not going to change our canon of scripture, the warning is about trying to remove anything from Revelation, or to add to it. This book stands alone in scripture as the most complete revelation from God about our destiny.

What this doesn't mean is that we can't discuss, comment or theorize about Revelation. In fact, having our opinions and letting our imaginations wander as to how these things could take place is a good thing because it will insert us into the narrative of this very real book. What we cannot do, however, is try to edit out parts of it we don't like because of our prejudices.

The concept of Jesus judging is a very touchy subject these days. People don't want a judge; they want to live their lives without God's input. That level of rebellion is what leads people to cut out the parts they don't like and leave what's convenient in this book.

No, we must surely own the fact that Jesus is not just a savior and also not just a judge; He is both. Jesus took on our shame and offered us eternal life but He is also coming back with full authority to judge and condemn those who have rebelled against His rightful leadership.

John ends his letter with the desire all believers should carry:

Come quickly, Lord Jesus.
Let your grace be upon us.

Don't forget to read Revelation this week!
Visit 10WeekBible.com for more resources including daily
podcasts, videos and more.

READING CHART

WEEK 1
- ☐ Day 1: Chapters 1-3
- ☐ Day 2: Chapters 4-7
- ☐ Day 3: Chapters 8-11
- ☐ Day 4: Chapters 12-15
- ☐ Day 5: Chapters 16-19
- ☐ Day 6: Chapters 20-22

WEEK 2
- ☐ Day 1: Chapters 1-3
- ☐ Day 2: Chapters 4-7
- ☐ Day 3: Chapters 8-11
- ☐ Day 4: Chapters 12-15
- ☐ Day 5: Chapters 16-19
- ☐ Day 6: Chapters 20-22

WEEK 3
- ☐ Day 1: Chapters 1-3
- ☐ Day 2: Chapters 4-7
- ☐ Day 3: Chapters 8-11
- ☐ Day 4: Chapters 12-15
- ☐ Day 5: Chapters 16-19
- ☐ Day 6: Chapters 20-22

WEEK 4
- ☐ Day 1: Chapters 1-3
- ☐ Day 2: Chapters 4-7
- ☐ Day 3: Chapters 8-11
- ☐ Day 4: Chapters 12-15
- ☐ Day 5: Chapters 16-19
- ☐ Day 6: Chapters 20-22

WEEK 5
- ☐ Day 1: Chapters 1-3
- ☐ Day 2: Chapters 4-7
- ☐ Day 3: Chapters 8-11
- ☐ Day 4: Chapters 12-15
- ☐ Day 5: Chapters 16-19
- ☐ Day 6: Chapters 20-22

WEEK 6
- ☐ Day 1: Chapters 1-3
- ☐ Day 2: Chapters 4-7
- ☐ Day 3: Chapters 8-11
- ☐ Day 4: Chapters 12-15
- ☐ Day 5: Chapters 16-19
- ☐ Day 6: Chapters 20-22

WEEK 7
- ☐ Day 1: Chapters 1-3
- ☐ Day 2: Chapters 4-7
- ☐ Day 3: Chapters 8-11
- ☐ Day 4: Chapters 12-15
- ☐ Day 5: Chapters 16-19
- ☐ Day 6: Chapters 20-22

WEEK 8
- ☐ Day 1: Chapters 1-3
- ☐ Day 2: Chapters 4-7
- ☐ Day 3: Chapters 8-11
- ☐ Day 4: Chapters 12-15
- ☐ Day 5: Chapters 16-19
- ☐ Day 6: Chapters 20-22

WEEK 9
- ☐ Day 1: Chapters 1-3
- ☐ Day 2: Chapters 4-7
- ☐ Day 3: Chapters 8-11
- ☐ Day 4: Chapters 12-15
- ☐ Day 5: Chapters 16-19
- ☐ Day 6: Chapters 20-22

WEEK 10
- ☐ Day 1: Chapters 1-3
- ☐ Day 2: Chapters 4-7
- ☐ Day 3: Chapters 8-11
- ☐ Day 4: Chapters 12-15
- ☐ Day 5: Chapters 16-19
- ☐ Day 6: Chapters 20-22

ABOUT THE AUTHOR

Darren Hibbs is the founder of the 10 Week Bible Study. He believes that the methodology of studying the Bible in this book can radically transform your life with God.

By filling your heart and mind with the Word of God first and foremost, you will better know God's heart than if your Bible knowledge comes primarily from sermons or even the commentary provided within this book. There is nothing more powerful for transformation than a people who know for themselves the Word of God.

Darren's heart burns to bring a message of hope to a lost and broken world through the immeasurable love of Jesus. It is his heart that the church will grow in love for God and embrace His love and power so that the lost will see and hear the good news about Jesus as they see it change us.

Darren writes regularly and can be reached at
www.DarrenHibbs.com

OTHER TITLES BY 10 WEEK BIBLE

Titles in Print & Digital Formats:
1 Samuel
2 Samuel
Esther
Daniel
John
Acts
Romans
Revelation

For a full and up-to-date list of titles in print, as well as for bookstore ordering information, visit 10WeekBible.com

FIND OUT MORE AT 10WEEKBIBLE.COM

10 Week Bible Study Podcast

If you have enjoyed this study, you may also enjoy the 10 Week Bible Study Podcast. This is a five day a week broadcast designed to help you get through each book of the Bible ten weeks at a time. It includes the reading of the entire book being studied once and helpful commentary to encourage your personal reading and study of God's Word.

You can listen to the podcast on any platform on the go or at home. For a list of easy links to subscribe to the podcast, visit 10WeekBible.com.

There, you can also subscribe to the broadcast on YouTube.

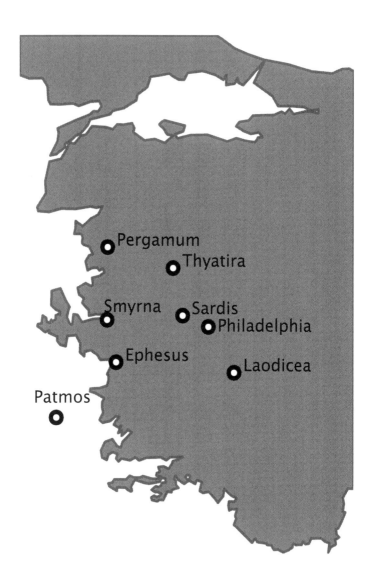